Activate Your Faith

Russ Johnston

PRESS

www.xulonpress.com

Dedication

∿∿

I n basic training for the Army Airborne, I bunked next to Grover Jonas, a soldier who never should have made it into the military. He stood barely 5'2", and weighed 110 pounds soaking wet. To graduate from basic we had to do twenty pull-ups. Grover was so small we had to lift him up to grab the bar so he could even begin. But Grover had the determination of six bulldogs, and though too small and too skinny, he became a paratrooper.

This book is dedicated to all the Grover Jonases who want to do great things for God, but have been told or who tell themselves they don't have what it takes.

The good news is this: God is for you. May this book be the "lift" you need to get moving in faith.

Contents

∿

Chapter 1

Activate Your Faith

∿

You may be a fan of the mega-faith stories of the Bible. I'm thinking of little David fighting the giant Goliath, courageous Daniel and the den of hungry lions, a worldwide flood and Noah's rescue. However, I find it easier to identify with other, smaller faith stories of the Bible. I like the one in which a seminary student borrowed an ax, and while using it to do volunteer work, lost the ax head in a river. Yet because of faith, the ax head floated (see II Kings 6:1-7). Or, how about the story of a woman with a serious medical problem? She'd worked with doctors for twelve years, and had gotten worse. Yet, as a result of her faith, healing came (see Mark 5:25-34). Or a young student's widow with two sons who had big bills. Her creditors said, "Pay up or we'll take your two sons as slaves." Faith bailed them out (see II Kings 4:1-7). Or the single mom with one son whose food supply was down to one pancake without toppings. Her plan was to make the pancake, eat it, then with her son die of starvation. But God worked because of her faith (see I Kings 17:8-16).

These "smaller" faith experiences resonate better with me because I've never seen myself as a potential Mountain Mover. When I was in the second grade my teacher told my mother I was the dumbest kid in the class. I spent two years in the fourth grade, and in high school was in the lower 50% of my class. Later, my high school football coach encouraged me to try out for the football team at Iowa State University. I won a scholarship, but my entrance reading comprehension score was in the fourth percentile! Can you see why I never put myself in the Mountain Mover category?

During college, another football player led me to a relationship with Jesus Christ. Since that time, I've seen God work and grow my faith, and life has become a wonderful adventure. An Iowa farm kid who flunked the fourth grade has spoken to all the cadets at the West Point of Taiwan, flown on a mission in Vietnam as a civilian while the war was in full force, had a seven-week speaking tour through South Africa, taught a seminar in Russia on biblical principles of doing business, and held an evangelistic rally for university students at the Governor's Mansion in Lincoln, Nebraska. I've been $478,000 in debt when interest was 23% and seen God deliver me. I've written a book that became a best seller. Best of all, I've seen scores of individuals come to know the Lord personally.

How did all this happen? Certainly not by my skill and ability. No, it was because of faith – faith in God's promises and God's provision. Through the years, God has helped me understand, not just how to grow my own faith, but how others can see their faith grow, too. In the pages ahead you'll read Scripture and read many stories of how people like you applied principles of living by faith to see their lives change.

These principles are best expressed in an experience a number of years ago centered on a growing family and a too-small house.

My wife and I had a problem. We had four children, a big dog, and needed a larger house than the raised ranch we owned. However, we weren't in a position to borrow any more money. Big need, little resources; that's a problem.

You see, a year earlier we had needed cash (I'd gone into selling real estate and was still adjusting to a commission-based income.) So, to generate what we needed, I refinanced the house we owned with a V.A. loan. Taking out the loan raised our house payment by a third, but we thought we could handle it, and the loan company did, too. So, we were maxed out on what we could pay, for housing but a bigger house would likely cost more, thus additional payments. What to do?

Prayer was the place to start. Next, my wife heard that a couple around the corner was getting a divorce and the wife was looking for a smaller house. We knew this house: six bedrooms, three and a half baths, two large family rooms, three fireplaces, a playroom – even a laundry chute and a safe. Later, as we passed their house while on a walk, we saw the "For Sale" sign in the yard. Half jokingly we looked at their very large house, and said to each other, "Maybe they would trade houses with us."

We made another loop around the block, and stopped again in front of the big house. Before we could give careful consideration to what we were doing, we knocked on their door, greeted our neighbor, and explained our idea of a house swap.

To our amazement, the woman became more excited as we talked. She invited us in to see her house. However, we both knew we didn't want to get attached to her house until we thought this had a chance of developing, so instead we invited her to look at our house. "My husband and I will come to look at your house as soon as he gets home," she told us. We hurried home to tidy up; in a little while we welcomed them. The wife quickly became excited. "That carpet will go wonderfully with my furniture!" she exclaimed.

The husband, however, peppered us with questions. "How much did you pay for those appliances? How old is the carpet? Does the refrigerator come with the house?" We could feel his resistance to the idea. However, as we talked, we discovered they also had a VA loan; we could assume each other's without anyone having to qualify. Plus, in spite of the fact that the value of the two houses was dramatically different, the amount of equity that we each had was more or less the same. In the days ahead, we actually did trade houses, loans and equities. We each paid half the real estate commission. With God's help, The Johnstons had room to spare!

However, our faith journey was only half completed. Besides a house twice the size of our old one, we now also had payments that were nearly twice the size of ones we currently struggled to meet. We prayed diligently that God would lower those enormous payments, but for an entire year, he didn't. (I don't remember how we made those payments, but by his grace we did, and we weren't late once.)

However, the last month of that year we received notice that our payments for the next year would be even higher – they had made a mistake in the initial calculations and had not taken out enough to pay the insurance and taxes. What to do?

As we sat at the kitchen table talking about the problem, my wife said, "Why don't we just pay the house loan off?" I was incredulous. "It's clear you do not understand real estate," I informed her. But her idea wasn't her idea; it was God's solution for us, spoken through her. In the days ahead the idea wouldn't let either of us go. Finally we agreed to pray that God would allow us to pay off the house in the next year. We prayed, but I have to admit it took me a full six months of praying before my faith had germinated to the point where I could say with total peace, "We are going to pay off this mortgage this year."

Things began to move. Besides real estate and speaking engagements, I had also begun to buy old houses to fix up and sell. That year I bought three houses to renovate and resell, and each one made a profit *four times more per house* than I had ever made before. The next year the profit margin on the houses I was renovating went back to the previous level. Clearly something God-generated happened during that year of trusting him for such a large sum of money.

Now, God kept working on our faith while he was providing the house money. When the wonderfully increased profit came in for the first house, it was very tempting to use it to make our house payments instead of putting it against the loan principal. After all, paying down the principal moved us toward a final pay-off, but it did nothing to lower our monthly payments. If God didn't come through with all we needed to pay off the loan, we were still going to be living under the same month-to-month financial pressure we'd already experienced for a year. But we took a deep breath, and applied the money to the loan. We chose to trust God's longer-range provision rather than invest in our own short-term security.

And He blessed. Almost a year to the day, we paid off the entire home loan.

This experience became one of hundreds in the years ahead for me and for those God allowed me to encourage as we saw God work by faith. I tell it because it shows God's power, and it shows the faith path that we're going to explore together in the pages ahead. Faith experiences follow four steps, and we'll learn together how these steps can be part of your faith journey:

- Choose God as the Object of Your Faith
- Make a List
- Decide
- Let Faith Germinate

Besides these steps, there are two perspectives that can help energize your growth in faith. These are:

- Grow Faith by Giving
- Align to the Will of God

Then, we'll close with a celebration of God's power at work as he encourages and sustains our faith. I trust you'll see through it all that the Lord can use ordinary people to move mountains as we learn to step out by faith.

Section I

Choose God as the Object of Your Faith

Chapter 2

Who Are You Trusting?

G od has many names: Creator, Counselor, Deliverer, Prince of Peace, Rock, Shepherd – the list could go on. Though all God's names are important, from a faith perspective there is one name so far above the others that it makes the others as big as one joint on one leg of a centipede! That name is this: Father. When his disciples said, "Teach us to pray," Jesus began, "Our Father..."

He himself prayed to God as his father. Remember Jesus in agony in the Garden of Gethsemane? He didn't ask for help from a distant sovereign entity; He cried, "*Abba*, Father..." (Mark 14:36) Seeing this example, Paul exhorts the Romans, "For you did not receive a spirit that makes you a slave again to fear, but you received the Spirit of sonship. And by him we cry, '*Abba*, Father.' The Spirit himself testifies with our spirit that we are God's children." (Romans 8:15-16) And again, "God sent him [Jesus] to buy freedom for us who were slaves to the law, so that he could adopt us as his very own children. And because you Gentiles have become his children, God has sent the Spirit of his Son into your hearts, and now can call God your dear Father. Now you are no longer a slave but God's own child. And since you are his child, everything he has belongs to you." (Galatians 4:5-7 NLT)

If God is our father, what kind of father is he? Many would say he's well-resourced, and certainly able to help us when we're in need. But do you believe he's also *willing* to help?

"Willing" is too weak, too tame, too passive to express God's attitude toward us. Listen to II Chronicles 16:9a KJV, "The eyes of the Lord run to and fro throughout the whole earth, to show himself strong in the behalf of them whose heart is perfect towards him..." He's not sitting behind a locked door, expecting you'll come banging on the door loudly enough to get his attention. He's out looking for you!

When I think of God looking for us to help and bless us, I think back to an experience a number of years ago when President Ronald Reagan came to visit the Air Force Academy. Because I volunteered to be one of the drivers in his motorcade, I got an up close and personal look at the Secret Service. Here's what I noticed. Even when I'd be standing directly in front of one of these agents, his eyes were constantly moving, up and down, back and forth looking for any movement out of the ordinary. I think this is how God looks at us. He's attentively watching, searching for any sign that we might want his involvement in our lives.

Why does He seek to aggressively to help us? It's because of his love for us. "As a father has compassion on his children, so the Lord has compassion on those who fear him." (Psalm 103:13) It is not what God *can* do, but what we believe he is *eager* to do, that inspires faith.

Do you see God as a generous, giving father, ready, eager, even pro-active to help you when you call on him?

Chapter 3

What Is Your God Like?

∿∿

If you believe in a God who doesn't hear you when you pray, you won't pray. What's the use? If you believe in a God who only answers righteous people's prayers – and you feel unrighteous – you won't pray.

"Our God is in heaven; he does whatever pleases him. But their idols are silver and gold, made by the hands of men. They have mouths, but cannot speak, eyes, but they cannot see; they have ears, but cannot hear, noses, but they cannot smell; they have hands, but cannot feel, feet, but they cannot walk; nor can they utter a sound with their throats. *Those who make them will be like them, and so will all who trust in them.* (Psalm 115:3-8)

A little church I once spoke to was seeking to raise about $150,000 for an education expansion to their building. Both their leadership and the fundraising group they had consulted considered this an ambitious goal. Their church had about 80 in attendance, and had met on the same little corner of their small Midwestern town for 40-50 years. As for giving, church members saw it as a responsibility, and something people were expected to do as part of the congregation.

When we began meeting to talk about faith and giving, I took a different view, and introduced the Scriptural idea that the God who owns the earth and all that is in it does not need our money. Giving,

I told them, is an act of worship, a privilege, and a means of blessing for us and for others.

Two weeks after this teaching session, people brought their pledges to the building campaign. They totaled, not $150,000, but nearly $475,000! When their concept of God changed, their giving changed, too.

To whom do you trust your life? Our natural tendency is to trust ourselves. If we simply do what comes naturally, we're going to rely on our own resources, abilities and know-how. We don't look to God because we have a mistaken idea of what he's like. For some, he's the Santa Claus in the Sky who will reward us with things if we're more nice than naughty. Or others see a high and mighty lawgiver who is remote from our daily concerns and care. Still others hold to the view that "God helps those who help themselves." They believe that God's gifts are limited by their own abilities and resource (never mind this 'verse' comes not from the Bible but Benjamin Franklin's *Poor Richard's Almanac!*)

Instead, we need to follow the challenge laid down in Hosea 6:3 NLT. "Oh, that we might know the Lord! Let us press on to know him! Then he will respond to us as surely as the arrival of dawn or the coming of rains in early spring." If we seek him, he promises that we will find him. He will come and show himself to us as sure as rain always comes in the spring.

Some turn away from trusting God with their lives because they believe he only involves himself in the "spiritual stuff" like salvation or church finances. However, the Bible tells us again and again this just isn't so. Look back to Hosea. He responds with spring rains that help the crops to grow. How spiritual is that? Or think about stories from the life of Jesus. He healed the sick, raised the dead, even calmed a storm. God's desire to work in our lives isn't limited to forgiving our sins and reconciling us to himself. He is just as concerned with our daily needs and cares as we are. Why else would he tell us to "cast our cares on him, for he cares for you?" Why else would he say, "God will supply all your needs according to his riches in glory in Christ Jesus?" Why else would he command us to "Pray about everything. Tell God your needs and don't forget to thank him when he answers?"

I believe this: our image of God determines how big our faith is and whether we are willing to exercise it. The beginning and end of living a life of faith will be limited only by how well you know the God who is good.

What pictures represent how you see God? What needs to change in your thinking about God to align your beliefs more closely to the real God who came to us in Jesus Christ?

Chapter 4

Three Bedrock Truths

∿∿

L isten carefully to this promise. "My God shall supply all your need according to his riches in glory in Christ Jesus." (Philippians 4:19 KJV) In this simple statement, we find what I think are the three bedrock teachings that guide us in living by faith. They are these:

1. "My God shall supply…" God is the resource of all our provision. We become so easily confused about the source of our needs being met. When in need, it's easy look first to government, people, institutions or credit cards. God uses these as instruments, of course, but they are not the source of supply. One woman who was unemployed said, "When I was getting those paychecks from my company every two weeks I got a little mixed up. I thought my company was my provider, so when I lost my job and those bi-weekly checks, I feared I'd also lost all my provision. Really, God was always my provider. It's just that for years he did it through those every-two-week checks. Now he's using different methods and frequency, but the fact that my needs are being met hasn't changed at all."

2. "…according to his riches in glory…" Just this morning in my Bible reading I came across this wonderful disclosure from God. He said, "If I were hungry I would not mention it

to you, for all the world is mine and everything in it." (Psalm 50:12 NLT) God's supply isn't based on the size of your need but on the enormity of his riches and his willingness to disburse them. In times of economic recession and abundance his supply stays stable and inexhaustible. In other words, God's bubble never bursts.

3. "...in Christ Jesus." We're invited to draw on God's abundant supply and blessing – not because of our goodness or our faithfulness or our church attendance, but because Jesus Christ lives in us. Because of Jesus' death and resurrection, God's arms are wide open to us; there is nothing between us anymore, no anger, no judgment, no retribution, no condemnation. Only grace, love and kindness. In fact, he insists we come to him boldly – confidently – to seek his help in time of need.

If you have any doubt this is true, listen to what King David says in Psalm 51. Remember, these words were written after Nathan the prophet had come to inform David of God's judgment against him because of his adultery with Bathsheba, and his murder of Uriah, her husband.

"Have mercy on me, O God, because of your unfailing love. Because of your great compassion, blot out the stain of my sins. Purify me from my sins, and I will be clean; wash me, and I will be whiter than snow. Don't keep looking at my sins. Remove the stain of my guilt. Restore to me again the joy of your salvation, and make me willing to obey you." (Psalm 51:1,7,9,12 NLT)

At the end of his confession David knew without a doubt God would stand by his word. David's repentance and God's character settled the issue between them forever. David spoke with confidence after he had done his part in confessing sin, and he had called on God to do his part, forgiving and restoring, "Then I will teach your ways to sinners, and they will return to you." (Psalm 51:13 NLT) God will bless and use you again, starting now.

Which of these three truths is most real to you? Which needs strengthening as a bedrock truth for you as you grow in faith?

Chapter 5

Abraham Shows the Way

God makes promises and then fulfills them wherever they are combined with our faith. Why do I say this? It's because God's Word said it first. "Does God…work miracles among you because you obey the law of Moses? Of course not! It is because you believe the message you heard about Christ. In the same way, 'Abraham believed God, so God declared him righteous because of his faith.'" (Galatians 3:5-6 NLT)

At age 75 Abraham received God's promises that he would become the father of many nations, with children as numerous as stars in the heaven or sand on the seashore. However, his circumstances mocked these promises. He had never had children when the promise was given because his wife was infertile. By the time the promise came again in the land God was giving Him, Sarah – even if she had ever been fertile – was 90 years old, and Abraham himself was 100 years old! It seemed to be too late. Yet Abraham's faith held strong.

How did he continue to believe?

First, He looked not at the circumstances, but at the character of God. ("He staggered not at the promise of God through unbelief; but was strong in faith, giving glory to God; and being fully persuaded that what he had promised, he was able also to perform." (Romans 4:20-21 KJV)

Second, he refused to cast away his confidence in God when the Lord told him to offer up Issac, the son who had finally been born. Under apparently hopeless circumstances he stood strong.

Abraham was not a super saint during all that time he waited. We have God's record that he lied, and he even tried to help God out, even though God neither needed or wanted his help. He was human but he held onto the promises through thick and thin.

After college I was a missionary to American servicemen on the island of Okinawa. God blessed the ministry, and a number of new Christians were growing in weekly Bible studies. One of the guys in the study heard about a Christian crusade in Tokyo that would involve as many as 30,000 people. Attending this could be great chance to help accelerate our growth! Now, how to get there? Flying was out of the question for enlisted men making $122 per month, so we booked third class berths on the Naha Maro for a 29-hour boat ride from Okinawa to the southern-most city in Japan. A round-trip ticket on the ship cost $28, and included all the rice and fish you could eat! Not glamorous, but it would get us to the conference.

The first night of the conference, we talked together about how much we'd enjoy seeing other Americans. The usher seating us took us to the top of the auditorium and seated us behind a white couple. When the first song ended, the man in front of us turned around, extended a handshake, and said "Hello, I'm Bill Bright, and this is my wife Vonette." I recognized him at once as the legendary founder of Campus Crusade for Christ International, and was amazed to meet him in such an unusual place.

Four days later we went to our ship for the trip back to Okinawa. However, we learned that a typhoon was headed for that coast, so our ship wouldn't be allowed to leave the port for at least two days. We were strapped for cash, and had no idea what to do but pray for direction.

Just then, the captain of our ship walked by. As it turned out, he spoke English and asked, "Are you waiting for typhoon to blow over so we can leave for Okinawa?" We were. "Why don't you just come and stay on the ship until we leave?" Since we had no alternative and no money, we followed him. As it turned out, instead of the economy berths we slept in on the way to Japan, he led us to first-

26

class beds and food, a clear improvement over the 5'6" x 18" mats, sand-filled pillows, and rice-and-fish diets we had paid for.

God can be trusted. We need Abraham's tenacious faith to anchor our faith in God's character rather than circumstances.

Do you let circumstances or God's character determine if you will have faith?

Chapter 6

Do You Want to Get or Grow?

∿

I knew of a book publisher who espoused a "throw 'em up against the wall and see what sticks" marketing philosophy. Here's what I mean. This publishing house would contract with as many authors as they could whose books were low-investment, and get books into print and into bookstores with only minimal marketing, then wait to see which "took off." When one would begin to sell, the publishing house would then shift marketing dollars to it and push to make it a best-seller.

You may be approaching prayer the same way. You've read God's promise in Mark 11:24. "Therefore I tell you, whatever you ask for in prayer, believe that you have received it and it will be yours." So, you begin to throw requests God's way, hoping that for some you may have "faith enough" to get God to answer. You're not sure how much faith is enough faith, but you take what you have and start asking – start throwing requests up against the wall – and hoping some of them stick and God answers.

Prayer in faith is not an inner conviction that God will fulfill our desires if only we believe enough. Faith isn't a possession. It's not something we own, like an idea or a feeling. And it certainly isn't a *"gimme gimmick."*

Faith is an aspect of a relationship. It always involves another person, and requires trust in that person to think and act in a certain way. Faith in God is a conviction about who He is, what He is like, and how He will respond to His children. Our faith needs to rest in the belief that God responds to us in line with his purposes, his promises and his power.

When he tells us to come to him in prayer in faith believing, he isn't simply out to provide a mechanism for getting our needs met and desires fulfilled. If simply functioning as a Great Vending Machine in the Sky was his purpose, there are far more efficient ways to dump goodness on us than by encouraging a prayer of faith. However, his intention is to develop a relationship with us – this was from the beginning his purpose in creating Adam and Eve, and it is his purpose for us today. Prayer was intended to be a vehicle for growing intimacy with God – for sharing our hearts with him, and inviting him to share his heart with us. And though the "things" that are exchanged as a result of this shared intimacy are important to our security and joy on earth, they are by-products, not the end results of praying in faith.

This is the spirit that drove Peter's instruction to "give all your worries and cares to God, for he cares about what happens to you." (I Peter 5:7 NLT) Prayer becomes real prayer when I'm talking with – and sharing my heart with – someone I believe genuinely cares what happens to me, someone who has already promised to help me in my time of need. It's that belief in God's unrelenting good-ness, his love, and his care that constitute the faith that makes prayer work.

Prayer done in this spirit is like this: a husband and wife have gone out for dinner on Friday nights as far back as they can remember. However, one Friday night she says, "Honey, I'm really bushed. How about if we stayed home tonight and eat here?" If there is no love relationship there could be a schism between them over this change. But if their hearts are blended together in love, you'd hear him respond, "Sweetie, I'm glad you told me. It isn't dinner out I really want; it's time with you." Giving and receiving come too easily when the relationship comes first.

Do you use prayer primarily as a tool to get your needs met? Or is it a loving interaction with someone you are seeking to love and trust more?

Chapter 7

Base Your Faith on God's Promises

∿

When our faith is small, our problems seem big. However, the reverse is also true: when faith is big, problems seem small. My faith grows quickest when I begin to focus on God and his immense promises! What God promises has to be the foundation of our belief.

Nehemiah is my example when I think of growing the kind of faith that shrinks my problems, because by anyone's estimation, his problems started large. In Nehemiah 1, he outlines the situation. As a captive in Persia, Nehemiah mourned over the desperate situation in his homeland of Israel. The walls of Jerusalem were broken down, and the gates that should have offered protection had been burned. The worship of foreign gods had become commonplace among those left in the country, and no one seemed to care. Big problems! No wonder the Scripture records that Nehemiah's response to these conditions was to weep, then fast and pray (see Nehemiah 1: 4). Sometimes in the face of large problems, we're tempted to stop right there – weeping, fasting, praying. What hope is there? But Nehemiah moved on, and his action changed weeping to faith. He reviewed what God had promised to his people, and how faithful He had been in keeping his promises (see Nehemiah 1:5-10). When we turn from our problems to focus on God – his character, attributes, faithfulness, mercy, grace, promise-keeping; faith begins to replace fear, just as it did for Nehemiah.

If you are new to the Scriptures, consider the list that follows a starting place. You'll find here some of the Bible passages that have been useful to my faith journey when problems looked big and my faith was small.

"His divine power has given us everything we need for life and godliness through our knowledge of him who called us by his own glory and goodness. Through these he has given us his very great and precious promises, so that through them you may participate in the divine nature. " (II Peter 1:3,4)

"Your promises have been thoroughly tested, and your servant loves them." (Psalm 119:140)

"God is not a man that he should lie, nor a son of man, that he should change his mind. " (Numbers 23:19)

"For no matter how many promises God has made, they are 'Yes' in Christ. (II Corinthians 1:20a)

"I am the bread of life. He who comes to me will never go hungry, and he who believes in me will never be thirsty." (John 6:35)

"I am the light of the world. Whoever follows me will never walk in darkness, but will have the light of life." (John 8:12)

"I am not alone. I stand with the Father, who sent me." (John 8:16b)

"I am the gate; whoever enters through me will be saved. He will come in and go out, and find pasture." (John 10:9)

"I am the good shepherd. The good shepherd lays down his life for the sheep." (John 10:11)

"I am God's Son." (John 10:36b)

"I am the resurrection and the life. He who believes in me will live." (John 11:25)

"I am the way and the truth and the life. No one comes to the Father except through me. " (John 14:6)

"I am in my Father, and you are in me, and I am in you." (John 14:20)

"I am the vine; you are the branches. If a man remains in me and I in him, he will bear much fruit; apart from me you can do nothing." (John 15:5)

Your Father wants you to take him at his word – to believe these promises, and to hold him to them. When you do, you'll find faith getting bigger and problems getting smaller.

Which of God's promises is the greatest "jumpstart" to your faith?

Chapter 8

God Plus Faith Equals Change

∿

If you opened the book of Acts in the New Testament, you'll find Christ-followers whose lives were on fire, full of adventure and possibility. They were constantly overcoming obstacles that appeared insurmountable. Their belief in Jesus transformed the way they lived. Their faith was not merely an add-on, but rather was central to their entire way of life. It overflowed in the lives of others in ways that were unimaginably transformational.

Do you want a life like that? It's what God wants for you. His intention is that our lives would be full of possibility and adventure. Where God is, there is life abundant. The Bible includes an amazing array of word pictures to stretch our minds and stir our imaginations about what God can do. There are jars of oil that just keep pouring and pouring, blind men that see, wayward sons returning home, bountiful harvests, legs once crippled now leaping, and prison doors flung wide open. Adults and children are pulled back from death to life. All of these things happen because God is powerfully present and inhabiting his people.

Many people listened to Jesus on those Galilean hillsides two thousand years ago, but not everyone saw Jesus the Messiah for who he was. What made the difference? It was faith. Those with faith got it. They saw Jesus for who he was and followed him. They saw themselves for who they really were in him. As a result, they performed miracles and healings in the lives of others, even though they were just common, untrained folks. Faith made the difference.

Look at just a few chapters from the Gospel of Mark, for instance. In chapter 5, after Jesus healed a woman who had been hemorrhaging for 12 years, he said to her, "Daughter, your faith has healed you. Go in peace and be freed from your suffering." (Mark 5:34) Later in the same chapter, Jesus goes with Jairus, who's daughter has died. "Don't be afraid," Jesus told Jairus, "Just believe." Then those with faith saw Jesus take the dead girl's hand and raise her to life.

In Mark 4, Jesus teaches his followers that the opposite is also true – the one who lacks faith will not see God do amazing things. Back in his hometown, Jesus didn't do the miracles he had been performing elsewhere. Why? "He could not do any miracles there, except lay his hands on a few sick people and heal them. And he was amazed at their lack of faith." (Mark 6:5-6)

On my first trip to Russia in 1991, four Russian interpreters helped our agricultural survey group to get around the country. On the last day, I decided to take a chance on challenging these interpreters – who by then had become our friends – with God's care for them.

"Would any of you like to come to America?" I asked, knowing from their conversations during the week that this was a dream for all. All four – a college professor, a grad student, a high-school English teacher and her 16-year-old daughter – all raised their hands with eagerness. I told them I couldn't work it out for them but the God of the Bible was looking for people to pray very special prayers. "Write down your request to go to America," I encouraged them, "and pray that God will provide a way." Three said nothing; the professor responded with a curt, "That isn't right!"

A year later a friend in Bloomington, Illinois called me to say there were four interpreters from the Russia trip visiting him and wondered if I'd like to see them. As it happened, a business group that followed our group to Russia had offered four interpreters a ten-day trip to America. So, to America came Ludmilla the English teacher, her daughter Julie, Luda the graduate student, and another Russian. The professor wasn't among them.

At the end of our visit, Ludmilla asked me to step outside on the porch; she had something important to tell me. She asked if I remembered challenging them to pray to God to get to America. I could tell she was looking for English words, and I wanted to jump in to say "...and God answered prayer!" Instead I waited. She looked up to heaven, raised her hand slightly, and said, "God is here." She understood the source of her provision.

God works most powerfully and clearly in those who believe that he *can and wants_to* work powerfully and clearly.

Would you have followed the professor's example, letting the largeness of your desire stop you from believing? Or is your faith more like the other three interpreters, who prayed anyway, even though the answer seemed impossible, and saw God work?

Section II

Make a List

Chapter 9

God Wants Us to Ask

∿

I want you to listen to these words of Jesus very carefully. "Then Jesus said to the disciples, 'Have faith in God. I assure you that you can say to this mountain, 'May God lift you up and throw you into the sea' and your command will be obeyed. All that's required is that you really believe and do not doubt in your heart. Listen to me! You can pray for anything, and if you believe, you will have it." (Mark 11:22-24 NLT)

Notice the progression. If you have faith in God, you will ask. Having a vague or abstract belief in the goodness of God is not enough. Faith must show itself in action, and that action is asking.

Jesus is always trying to get us to ask God. In the command we just read, he says, "Listen to me! You can pray for anything, and if you believe, you will have it." In John 15 he explains, "You didn't choose me. I chose you. I appointed you to go and produce fruit that will last, so that the Father will give you whatever you ask for, using my name." (John 15:16 NLT) He places no limits on what we can ask for. In fact, he seems to be trying to explode the limits that we place on ourselves and our own requests.

However, I hear these objections to asking:

- I can't pray for that because I feel so greedy.
- I'm not worthy enough to ask.

- God loves me so much that if I need anything He will give it without my asking.
- I'm happy where I am. If I prayed and didn't get an answer then I might be unhappy.
- It's too much effort to change what I am doing now.
- I don't want to take the time to think through my needs.
- God is not interested in the small stuff.
- I can't see how God could answer, so I don't ask.

Even in the face of objections like these, Jesus says we should ask, because asking is what faith looks like in action. If we have a correct image of God, we will ask.

A single mom I met in Phoenix was a Realtor, and when the bottom dropped out of the economy, her income bottomed out too, so she left Phoenix and moved in with her brother in San Diego. She gave a good portion of her furniture away and said goodbye to her home.

A few months later when we talked she told me the bank had an offer on her house in Phoenix, but they had not made a decision to sell yet. "I'd love to have that house back," she told me.

"Has the house been officially repossessed from you yet?" I asked. She said it hadn't. "Why don't you pray – tell God your desire to live in the house – and then call the bank and ask if you could just move back in?" She had never thought of this. Live in the house without being able to make payments on it? Surely that couldn't be possible. However, since she had nothing to lose, she made the call. The bank representative she spoke with said, "It's your house; you can do what you want." So she moved back into the house. She has lived there eleven months without making a house payment, paying real estate taxes, or buying insurance. To get the scope of this provision, her payments were about $1140 a month, with taxes and insurance extra.

I called two nights ago to check on her. This story was amazing enough I wanted to follow it. She reported, "I just talked to the people at the bank. They said there had been an offer from someone to buy the house, but it had fallen through. They said to stay put and when and if they did repossess the house, I would still have ninety days to move out."

Sometimes we don't have because we simply don't ask.

What's standing in the way of you taking a faith step to ask?

Chapter 10

Power of a List

ᵕᕦᕤ

Your faith will stay inactive until it finds a focus. I've found the quickest way to create a focus for faith is by a making a list. Here's what I mean. In Hebrews 11:1 we're told that faith is the "substance" – the building material – of things we hope for, those dreams inside us planted by God that only he can make possible. Making a list energizes those hopes with faith.

Do this: make a list of what you would like to be doing or have accomplished in three months if resources of any kind were no problem. Write what has been on the back burner of your mind from a week to ten years. In fact, go ahead – write some of those right now:

1.
2.
3.
4.
5.
6

Now, pray over this list until you can recall it easily. Then, put the list away. Let God work and your faith germinate. Then, look at your list in three months. You can expect God's response because he promised in Psalm 34:8, "Taste and see that the Lord is good." It's at his invitation that you test him. Making a list of faith goals is your way of responding to his invitation.

Remember, the only limits on your list should be God's resources, not yours. It's him you are putting to the test, not you. Do some goals require financial resources? God owns the cattle on a thousand hills. Is it health you need? Jesus came to heal all our diseases. Test him – he's inviting you to.

To make things even more interesting, write on a slip of paper what you want Jesus to change in your life. Pray over the list, whether it is filled with big requests or small ones. Then put it in an envelope, seal it, and mail it to a friend, asking that friend to mail it back to you in three months or so.

I've done this many times in seminars. People have reported, "I made the list and then prayed over it, just like you asked us to. Then I forgot about it (or maybe lost it) but found it a year later. Everything on the list had come to pass."

God wants you to exercise faith; you know you need to get an objective. But what objective? Old Testament leader Nehemiah gives us one piece of direction. I introduced him to you earlier as one of my faith heroes. Now, let's look at his story in greater depth.

"In late Autumn of the twentieth year of King Artaxerxes' reign, I was in the fortress of Susa. Hanani, one of my brothers came to visit me with some other men who had just arrived from Judah. I asked them about the Jews who had survived the captivity and about how things were going in Jerusalem.

They said to me, "Things are not going well for those who returned to the province of Judah. They are in great trouble and disgrace. The wall of Jerusalem has been torn down, and the gates have been burned.

When I heard this I sat down and wept. In fact, for days I mourned, fasted and prayed to the God of heaven." (Nehemiah 1:1-4 NLT)

Nehemiah knew God had to work something deep in him before God would do a big work through him. What came next is an amazing faith story of God's provision for Nehemiah to actually return to the land of Israel and rebuild the walls of Jerusalem – in a trip underwritten by his captor, the King of Persia!

When King Artaxerxes, who Nehemiah served as cupbearer, asked why Nehemiah seemed depressed, Nehemiah didn't hedge. He clearly expressed his specific concern: "The city where my ancestors are buried is in ruins and the gates have been burned down." The King asked about a remedy, and once again, Nehemiah got specific. "Send me to Judah," he said, "to rebuild the city of my fathers!"

Nehemiah had a very concrete faith objective. Notice that the objective didn't come from a heavenly revelation, complete with flashing lights and smoke. Nor was there a booming voice from the clouds with a "thou shalt..." vision. There wasn't much mystical at all. While catching up with old friends, he heard about a situation that concerned him, and a faith objective was born.

On my twelfth or thirteenth trip to Russia I heard about the 21 churches God had raised up. As we heard how God was blessing, they shared excitedly about gathering children for three-day Vacation Bible Schools, and how ready these children were to learn about Christ. It came to my mind that these churches needed a Bible Camp. I talked with a pastor about it but he didn't respond positively. "You Americans have all the big ideas, but we wind up having to support them." I thought, "He's right." I would have abandoned the idea, but before I left Russia, God impressed me that he wanted me to keep pursuing the idea of a camp. So, I told the pastor to start looking for a location and I would raise $100,000 for it.

Because I knew nothing about camping, the next year I took George Cheek, director of Maranatha Bible Camp in North Platte, Nebraska, with me to provide counsel and direction We looked at sites, talked and prayed but no direction came clear. However, the following year, a half-built lodge with some land was found and the camp was started.

To complete my commitment to provide $100,000, I first began asking for help from others in America, but the idea didn't reso-nate. (One person gave $1000.) I prayed and God spoke to my heart, "Providing $100,000 for the camp is the right goal, but your plan to get there is wrong. I want *you* to give the money yourself." It took me three years to generate the money through buying and flipping houses, but there is now a functioning, fulltime Bible camp to serve those 21 churches. Like Nehemiah, when my concern became a commitment, God moved.

What concerns for yourself or others are driving you to prayer? Which of these might be a faith objective for your list?

Chapter 11

Should We Ask for Ourselves?

∿

I know people who believe asking for things for ourselves is a primitive form of prayer, reflecting a selfish spirituality, while intercession for others reflects higher spirituality. This is unbiblical thinking. God has much to give and we have great need. Prayers that bring our needs to God connect us to his generous nature.

That's why Jesus told his disciples, "Ask and it will be given to you; seek and you will find; knock and the door will be opened to you. For everyone who asks receives; he who seeks finds; and to him who knocks, the door will be opened." (Luke 11:9-10) Notice this command doesn't say, "Ask that others' needs be met." There's no limiting condition on which requests we are to bring to God. Charles H. Spurgeon once said, "Whether we like it or not, asking is the rule of the kingdom." Asking keeps us aware of our total dependence on God, and reminds us to be continually inviting him into every moment of our lives.

It's not an insult to God to come asking. Saint Theresa of Avila once said, "You pay God a compliment by asking great things of him." Indeed, James tells us, "You do not have because you not ask God." (James 4:2b) A realtor friend of mine told me that this verse changed how she thought about a house she had listed that had had no activity in weeks. She'd done many things to generate interest, but one thing she hadn't done was ask God for help. "So I did," she told me, "and in the next week there was activity on the house. In fact one lady who called about it said God had told her to look at the house."

Other people matter to God, and he wants us to look to him to meet their needs. But God is just as interested in our growth in trust and dependency on him. That's why we need to ask for what we need and what we desire. He delights to respond.

Ephesians 6:18 tells us, "Pray in the Spirit on all occasions with all kinds of prayers and requests. With this in mind, be alert and always keep on praying for all the saints." Did you notice the four "all's" in the passage – *all occasions, all kinds, always and all the saints*? How much of our lives are to be brought to God? We're pretty safe in assuming that all of it is.

Once after sharing this verse with a group, I handed out 3x5 cards and asked them to write down their needs for the coming week. I encouraged them in the spirit of *all* not to edit the needs list; simply write them all down. The next week we reported on God's answers.

Eric, a foreman at a roofing company had problems getting employees to come to work on Fridays. His need list said, "Need enough employees to show up and put in a good day's work on Friday so I can get paid." On Friday all his employees came, and worked hard enough to be done by 5:00 – and Eric was paid. Randy, an alcoholic with 26 months of sobriety had not been able to lead his AA meeting for several weeks because of the workload of the harvest season. He told God how much it meant to him to attend those Tuesday and Thursday meetings and wrote, "Would like to be there for AA meetings." Without telling his boss about his prayer, the boss told him for two weeks in a row to go home early on Tuesdays and Thursdays.

Praying "on all occasions with all kinds of prayers always for all the saints..." means we are free to ask as broadly as life itself. That includes problems, joys, temptations and struggles. Let God in on your everyday life, your work, your bill-paying, your leisure time, your shopping, your doctor visits, and your time with friends. Welcome God right into the middle of your sometimes mundane, usually busy, occasionally stressful, and always complex life.

What concerns or desires for yourself have you been reluctant to bring to God?

Chapter 12

Short-Term Prayers

∿

L et me suggest three ways of praying that may provide you with a useful framework. I think in term of short-term, medium-term and long-term prayers.

I sometimes think of prods to short-term prayers as "God's pager." Think about it. Someone's pager goes off in a room full of people. The person gets up immediately, leaves the room, and answers the call. Something needed immediate attention, and that "beep, beep, beep" sent the wake-up call.

Anxiety can be God's pager, alerting us that it is time to talk to him about a situation that's worrying us. That's why he instructed us, "Be not anxious about anything, but in everything, by prayer and petition, with thanksgiving, present your requests to God. And the peace of God, which transcends all understanding, will guard your hearts and your minds in Christ Jesus." (Philippians 4:6-7) If, instead of wallowing in anxiety, or condemning ourselves when we feel anxiety, we were to use anxiety as a pager system to push us to prayer, we'd find ourselves experiencing more of the peace God promised.

I have notebooks full of short-term prayers. On Sunday or Monday night I make a list of everything I can think of that I would like God's help with in the coming week. Sometimes I have eight-to-ten things; sometimes 40-50. My list might look like this:

- Help me get the credit card mistake resolved
- Who should repair the lawnmower
- Should I plant perennials this year
- Help me spend enough time preparing for Bible study
- Clean out the garage
- Leave earlier for work on Wednesday to beat the detour traffic
- Write my friend in prison
- Check on airline tickets to Portland

I pray over this list just once, when I am making it. At the end of the week when I am making next week's list I review the list, give thanks for the answers. Some of the ones that weren't answered will be on the list for the next week. You will be thrilled at how God has helped.

A lady from North Carolina called me to ask about making a prayer list. "I just can't think of what to put on my list," she told me. We talked about anxiety as God's pager, but she still couldn't see it. "How anxious do I need to be in order to pray?" she asked.

In response, I shared some of my current requests for that month. From this list, it was easy to see that there's no need to edit your "cares" for intensity. Big ones, little ones, boring ones, emotional ones, even confused ones – all are reasonable subjects for prayer if we are seeking to live in peace.

Is God alerting you through some concern in your life? What's keeping you from calling him immediately?

Chapter 13

Medium-Term Prayers

∿

I consider medium-term prayers a way to focus on things for which I need direction, or need a decision about, in the next couple of months. A lot of these involve other people, and how they act or react to a situation. Some have to do with things I need or want but have no idea how to get.

I believe James had some of these same things in mind when he wrote in James 4:1, "What is causing the quarrels and fights among you? You want what you don't have, so you scheme and kill to get it. You are jealous for what others have, and you can't possess it, so you fight and quarrel to take it away from them. And yet the reason you don't have what you want is that you don't ask God for it."

I believe all of us have gone over and over these wars in our minds to no avail except anger, frustration, envy, lust and a host of other bad things. Instead we should have simply prayed.

Here are items on a current medium-term list:

- Income tax right, honest and as cheap as legal
- Teeth – should I change dentist for the new work
- When to go see my kids in North Carolina and Portland
- Get more motivated on writing
- How to handle future investments
- What to do with the money from house sale. Should I diversify?

- That my kids and grandkids would see your mighty works for themselves
- Psalm 119:81 – I expect help because you promised it
- Help me be a big risk taker
- How to be more of God's servant and obey
- Give me a new small group to be involved with
- Heal my leg – help me to do something everyday that will help it
- More speaking. I volunteer to be available.

I have 30 entries on this quarterly prayer page. I pray over this list twice or three times a week. I leave space between lines so I can record answers or progress.

A few weeks ago I added this item to my prayer list, "Up the cash flow." Shortly after, I was flying home from North Carolina and ready for the last leg of the trip, from Chicago to Des Moines. We were boarding the 4:12 p.m. flight when an announcement came that the plane was overbooked. "We'll give $400 to anyone willing to delay," the attendant said. I thought, "Why not? What's four hours?" However, there were ten people who had volunteered ahead of me and the plane was boarding. I decided to board, but going down the ramp I prayed, "God, if you want me to have a free ticket, work it out." We were all buckled in when the flight attendant came on the microphone. "We have a problem, " she said. "There is a little girl on the plane whose dad couldn't get on because of the overbooking. We are offering $400 for anyone who will give him their seat." I stood up immediately and said, "I'm the one." The people in the plane cheered.

I got my $400 voucher, a $15 meal ticket and a boarding pass for the 8:40 p.m. flight to Des Moines. Praise God! But as I reached for the voucher, the ticket agent leaned over the counter and said quietly, "If you want to get another voucher, we are overbooked for this 8:40 flight, too. Come at 8:00." Of course I arrived at 8:00, and receive another $400 travel voucher, a $15 meal ticket, and a voucher for lodging at the Chicago Hilton.

Before leaving the ticket counter, I asked about the time for the next day's flight to Des Moines. The counter attendant said there were two: 6:00 a.m. and 8:40 a.m.. I chose the 8:40; those who chose 6:00 a.m. went ahead of me to get booked on the flight, and left the area. As the two of us who had chosen the 8:40 worked on our tickets, an announcement came that the 8:40 for the following morning was (yes, you're reading it right) *overbooked*. Of course the two of us still at the counter volunteered to wait and received our $400 voucher – that was now $1200 in vouchers for me, remember? – and got boarding passes for the 1:05 flight the next day. I noticed there was a flight at 10:45 in the morning and asked if I could get on stand-by, just in case. No problem. As it turned out, the 1:05 was cancelled due to bad weather, but by then I was already safely in Des Moines – the 10:45 stand-by ticket had worked wonderfully. After a great night's rest at the Hilton I was home just a few hours later than I planned, and $1200 richer.

Later as I was going over my monthly prayer list I noticed on the list, "Up the cash flow." I know those vouchers weren't cash, but they sure work like cash when you fly as much as I do.

Once I traded in my pickup and accidentally left one of my prayer notebooks under the seat. A couple of months later I received a package that contained the notebook, with this note: "I found this under the seat. Thought you might like it back. This is the most unusual prayer book I have ever seen." It may have been, but if we want our faith to grow, we can do no better than to make prayers of faith a daily practice.

What do you see ahead in the next three months? How might these opportunities and concerns become medium-term faith requests for you?

Chapter 14

Long-Term Prayers

ᴧᴧ

Today's pressing needs make a starting point to learn about praying by faith. But I've found great power in also making a list of long-term faith requests. These may not happen immediately in the way requests for money to pay this month's orthodontist bill may. However, as faith matures, we also want to be sure we're moving toward a future that's built on faith. For me, having a list of long-term requests is a good way to build that faith-anchored future.

When writing long-term requests, I use these guidelines:

- Word your request so that it feels right to you
- State the end result, not the means of achieving it
- Eliminate the word "want"
- Include yourself in your request
- Phrase the request in the positive
- Word your request in the now as though it has already come to pass.

Here are some samples to get you started.

Relationships

I pray and allow my relationship with _____ to be _____ (relaxed, supporting, open or mutually beneficial).

I pray and allow myself to live, accept or forgive _____.

I pray and allow _____ to have what he/she wants for himself/ herself.

General Health and Well-Being

I pray and allow myself to achieve and maintain my ideal weight of _____.

I pray and allow myself to enjoy a regular exercise routine.
I pray and allow myself to enjoy being a non-smoker.

Financial and Career

I pray and allow myself to be paid well for doing what I love.
I pray and allow myself to feel at peace, like I have all the time in the world.
I pray and allow myself to have a net income of _____ or more a month.
I pray and allow myself to have _____.

God and Outreach

I pray and allow myself to be a strong finisher in my Christian life.
I pray and allow myself to continually be involved with outreach to non-Christians.
I pray and allow myself to grow in my love for the Lord.
I pray and allow myself to _____.
I don't share these long-term requests with many people. I pray over them until they are fixed in my mind. I look at them a couple of times a year to see the answers or let God give me some correction along the journey of life.

A number of years ago, a Christian organization I worked for asked me to lead their ministry with college students at the University of Nebraska, and to supervise five or six other ministries located in the region. I had just spent several months asking God for his leading about how he wanted to use my life. God's answer. "My true disciples produce much fruit. This brings great glory to my Father." (John 15:8 NLT) I wondered how God would fulfill this direction during my time in these student ministries.

When I reached the University of Nebraska, some of the students and I began to pray every morning at 6:00 a.m. in a dorm parking lot, asking God to help us reach the campus with His gospel. But as we prayed, our scope seemed to naturally expand. Along with prayers for the University of Nebraska, we also began asking God to use us on other campuses around the area. After a while someone came up with a map of the Midwest – Nebraska, Iowa, Missouri, Kansas – and we put yellow pins marking the location of every campus where God might use us to take the gospel, campuses like the University of Missouri, Kansas State, Kansas University, Missouri State University, Central College in Pella, Iowa, and more.

During the next years there was a movement of God. One college professor from the University of Nebraska changed jobs and moved to the University of Missouri, taking two students with him, and agreeing together they would focus their efforts in this new place on reaching students for Christ. Other students transferred to other schools to begin similar outreaches. Students going on to graduate work looked first at schools with no visible gospel outreach so they could be lights in the darkness there. A businessman in Iowa who lost his job at a trucking firm took a job with the Billy Graham office in Omaha, and stayed on specifically to do community outreach. With these and other movements of God, at the end of four years there were seventeen campus or community outreaches underway.

God had a passion and a plan to reach students with His truth, and He chose to use us to accomplish it, I believe, because I asked him for direction and a promise. He gave both, and was faithful to both. We need to start – not with our own plans – but by seeking God for His purposes and promises and then step out in confidence.

What are your long-term desires and concerns? Are they part of your prayer list?

Chapter 15

Asking Again

∿

S ometimes our faith objective can come from a concern that once seemed crucial to us, but of late has lost its steam.

As a young man, Moses had a concern for his Israeli brothers who were captives in Egypt. One day when he was visiting them, he saw an Egyptian knock a Hebrew to the ground. After checking to be sure no one was watching (Moses was no fool!) he killed the Egyptian in retaliation, and hid his body in the sand. However, Pharaoh found out and ordered that Moses be put to death. Moses ran for his life to the land of Midian, married a Midianite girl, and settled into sheepherding. So much for trying to save his people!

Forty years later, God came to Moses in a burning bush and re-awakened the objective that had initially presented itself through Moses' concern for the Hebrews. It's interesting that there was nothing wrong with Moses' initial objective; he wanted a better life for the Hebrews, a life free from Egyptian cruelty. However, he'd gone about answering the concern the wrong way. Killing one Egyptian was not God's method!

God did have a method, however, and it was larger, grander, and immeasurably more effective than the method Moses employed. God's plan took Moses straight to the top of the food chain, not to the bottom, where he had elected to start initially. God's method took him to a decision-maker who could with one stroke of a pen, or one spoken command, set free the children of Israel. And, in matching

Moses with Pharaoh, God set up a situation in which His glory could be seen in all of Egypt, an impact far greater than Moses could have ever imagined.

God's method and Moses' methods were different as night and day, but their objective was the same. Maybe for you, the concern that drove you was, in fact, God's clear faith objective for you; it was simply the methods you chose that didn't reflect His ways. It could be His methods were bolder than yours – and you've needed to grow into greater reliance on Him so you could step out by faith with steps the size of His.

Do you remember the sixteen-year-old Russian girl from an earlier chapter who, along with three other interpreters, learned to ask God for a trip to America and see Him provide? She went on to graduate from college and marry, and along with her new husband, worked and saved to buy a car. However, just as they were ready to make the purchase, an explosive round of inflation hit the Russian economy, and overnight the equivalent of $100,000 was now worth only $100. She said, "We were ready to buy a car, and the next day that same amount of money would only buy a pair of shoes."

As she told me about this disappointment, the Spirit prompted me to respond, "You did a good job saving for the car – that was not wrong. And the goal of having a car wasn't wrong. Will you ask God for a car and see what he does?" The circumstances had so disheartened her she only shrugged her shoulders so I had no idea where my suggestion would end.

Two years later at a dinner for Russian officials, this young woman was one of the interpreters. At the end of the banquet, she stood, and asked, "May I say a few words?" She told about her experience of losing the money to buy a car. Then she said, "Russ goaded me into praying for another car. God answered, and if you would like to see the car it is right now parked in front of the hotel."

What concerns called to you years ago? What did you once think was worth fighting for, but abandoned when your attempts to bring change met with failure?

Section III

Decide

Chapter 16

Quantifying Prayers

∿

When Jesus taught his disciples to pray, he instructed them to say, "Give us *this day* our *daily bread*." *This day* – that's when the bread should come; in other words, a time quantifier to the request. And *daily bread* – that's how much bread; in other words, a quantifying amount added to the request.

Often our prayers are just too general to serve as activators for faith. If we could zip to heaven and read God's prayer book for ourselves, we might have trouble figuring out which of the requests actually came from us. For example, "help us be better Christians" or "please meet all my needs." Of course God wants to do these things, but faith grows when we can recognize that he's responded to us, when we can see he's been at work. Recognizing God at work is so much easier when the prayer instead is, "Help us begin four new Bible studies this year, with at least six people in each." Or perhaps, "Please provide the house payment by Tuesday."

Jesus gave the "quantifier" principle again in one of his parables. "Then, teaching them more about prayer, he [Jesus] used this story: 'Suppose you went to a friend's house at midnight wanting to borrow three loaves of bread...'" (Luke 11:5 NLT) The qualifier of time? Midnight – not just sometime. The qualifier of amount? Three loaves - not just bread.

Our faith will grow faster when we quantify our prayers. We'll then recognize when God answers and give him the praise he deserves.

I was just starting out in ministry to students and was glad to be assigned to the University of Nebraska, and to other nearby campuses. I had responsibility, but no car to travel to Nebraska from Colorado where I was living. In talking with my boss, he recommended I get a nine-passenger station wagon, since I'd be transporting students most of the time for my ministry. This made sense, but since I had no money and couldn't go shopping, I spent my time praying for the station wagon. God seemed to be telling me to be even more specific, so I asked not just for the nine-passenger station wagon, but a blue one – and a new one! I prayed until I not only had peace about this particular car, but I could actually see myself driving it.

A college buddy found out about my vehicle-less predicament, and offered me his six-year-old Chevy with 80,000 miles on it. That was easy to refuse. A week later another Christian friend stopped me. "Russ, I heard about your need, and God spoke to me tonight that I should give you my two-year-old Volkswagen." Time had almost come to move to Nebraska, and I still had no vehicle, so I was tempted, but as I prayed, God gave no peace, so I refused it. "But God spoke to me..." Bob argued. I decided to stick to the leading God had given *me* – and the car wasn't new and wasn't blue.

Friends who were headed east provided a ride to Nebraska when the time came. Soon after I began meeting a small team of the University of Nebraska students and some businessmen in Lincoln who cared about this outreach. A car was high on the prayer list.

After three weeks, one of the businessmen called to tell me he'd heard there was a hail storm in Omaha, and some new cars had been slightly damaged. He wondered if I would like to go with him and look at them. We found only two – a brown one, and *a blue nine-passenger station wagon*. The businessman put down the 5% they wanted to hold the blue one for a month until we could get financing arranged. But as we prayed, gifts for the car started coming in. One month to the day of finding the car we went to Omaha to claim it, with not just the purchase price in hand, but an extra $100 that turned out be necessary to pay for a fee we hadn't anticipated. God provided all we needed before we knew we needed it. Before we took the keys, we joined hands in a circle in the dealership and thanked God for his faithfulness.

Praying so specifically and visualizing the answer by faith changed my prayer and faith life.

What requests on your list are so general you would hardly know if God had answered them? How can you quantify them?

Chapter 17

Faith, Not Slogans

∿∿

A faith goal that isn't quantified is just a slogan.

"I'm praying for a vacation." That's a slogan.
"I'm praying for a great vacation for my family this summer." That's quantified.

"I want to lead someone to Christ." A slogan.
"I'm praying to lead one person to Christ this year." That's measureable, and God can respond to that kind of focused faith.

S uccess in your faith doesn't come by magic or hocus pocus, but focus.

Focus matters because God doesn't answer vague prayers – or if He did, we'd never recognize the answers when they came. (After all, what does "bless our church" really look like?) When Bartimaeus, a blind man, came running after Jesus he cried, "Jesus, Son of David, have mercy on me." (See Mark 10:46-52) Although most people assumed Bartimaeus was seeking healing for his blindness, Christ asked, "What do you want me to do for you?" Jesus seeks specific requests to answer, not general ones to "have mercy," Bartimaeus said, "Rabbi, I want to see," Jesus replied, "Your faith has healed you," and Bartimaeus' eyes were opened.

My first trip to Russia wasn't intended as a ministry trip. I went with an agricultural group, and would be hosted by government officials. But I made up a private faith list anyway. One item on the list was to have the privilege of leading someone to Christ; another item was to be able to give away one of my faith books to a recipient of God's choice.

During a long layover in Frankfort, another traveler and I had the privilege of leading two East Indians to the Lord. One faith request granted!

The book recipient didn't appear as easily. During our two weeks of visiting farms and agricultural factories, there was barely time to keep up the pace, let alone make relationships. But on Day Thirteen, the answer appeared. I was to give it to an English professor we had met at the Agriculture Institute in Novgorod, and I did.

Two months later, a friend of mine in the cranberry industry invited me to go back to Russia with him – he was out to buy 2000 ton of cranberries. On that visit, I was able to reconnect with the English professor who had received my book. What had God intended with that gift? As it turned out, the professor had not just read the book, but gone on to translate it into Russian. Because her typewriter was broken and no parts could be found, she had written the translation out in long hand!

Here's the point. When you set a goal, challenge yourself with the words, "Be more specific." Keep repeating this until your goal is crystal-clear and measurable. By doing this you'll dramatically increase your chance of achieving the desired result by faith.

Is there one faith goal you might adjust to make it more specific?

Chapter 18

Right-Sizing Faith Goals

∿

Romans 14:5 offers wisdom to help us set faith goals. It directs, "Each one should be fully convinced in his own mind." Though this passage is directed toward how we determine our convictions, it has clear application to our convictions about faith.

If your faith goal is too small, you may go ahead and do it without God. Where's the faith in that? (I actually "check" my faith goals by asking, "If God didn't work, would there be any way this could happen?") However, there can be a problem on the other end of the continuum, too. Your faith goal can be too big. If it is, your mind, soul and spirit may not come together in agreement that results in the certainty of faith. Or, when God works, you may not be able to receive the answer with joy.

Here's what I mean. In response to faith, one man I know received a Cadillac. However, he told me later he only drove it at night because he didn't want the neighbors to think he was rich. The Lord had provided, but there was no celebration or joy in his provision because the recipient wasn't internally in agreement with a picture of himself owning a Cadillac and being okay.

In another circumstance, Tom, a rancher, called to discuss whether or not he should pray that he could trade their 500-cow, 2300-acre ranch in Colorado for a 1000-cow ranch in the Northwest. I didn't see anything wrong with the request. He called back in three months overjoyed, reporting that he had traded, and for a 1200-cow, 23,000 acre ranch in British Columbia.

The lesson from these two stories is this: the largeness of the faith goal isn't the limiter on what God can do. *The limiter is what outcome you can live with peacefully.* In the first case, the Cadillac came, but peace and joy didn't accompany it because the requester's mind wasn't fully convinced he could enjoy this gift without embarrassment or guilt. In the second, Tom and his wife were settled in their minds that a larger ranch would be a wonderful gift from a gracious generous Father who loved to bless them – and someone they wanted to bless in return.

How long should you pray for a goal? I use this pattern for prayers of faith:

1. Pray and confess it in your heart and mind first.
2. Pray and confess it out loud when you're alone.
3. Pray it over and over whenever.
4. Pray it until your words, your heart and your spirit agree.
5. Pray it until harmony comes. God will bear witness with your spirit and you will have peace that passes understanding.

Imagine yourself having received what you're asking God for. Do you see yourself happy and peaceful, or uncomfortable? What would need to be adjusted in the picture for you to see yourself at peace?

Chapter 19

Stumbling Block of "Means"

∿

I have never believed that I brought anything special to a walk of faith. However, I have always been willing – willing to say yes, willing to step out, willing to keep moving when I couldn't see how God was going to work. More of the time than not, I couldn't see how God would work out what he was calling me to do. Like Abraham, who received God's call to "go to the land I will show you" I didn't usually know where that final destination was going to be.

However, I gave up long ago needing to know *how* God would work before I was willing to believe he *would* work. My job was to believe him for the end; his job was to provide the means. It's the means that becomes a faith-stumbling block for many. Even Zacharias, father of John the Baptist, stumbled over the "means" question. When he heard from an angel that he was to be a parent in his old age, he responded, "How can I know this will happen? I'm an old man now, and my wife is also well along in years. How can this be?" God responded, "My words will certainly come true at the proper time." (Luke 1:18,20 NLT) The how is God's problem; deciding the goal is ours.

Jeff is a dear friend who is currently an inmate in a maximum security prison in Comstock, NY. One of our commitments is to spend Christmas together. During our visit last Christmas, I asked Jeff about his faith goals for the year.

He thought a moment, and said, "I'm teaching GED classes here in the prison, but most of my students are just going through the motions. They don't really have a heart to graduate." So we joined hands and prayed for three eager students by April 30, four months away.

By April 30, he had none! So, I suggested that it's okay to change the time qualifiers we put on requests, but not the requests. God promises to give us what we seek, and He promises His timing is perfect. However, that doesn't always mean His view of perfect timing matches ours. We agreed to keep praying.

On August 1 I got a letter from Jeff. The prison had dedicated a room for GED classes and decided to provide a teacher from the outside. Ten students had signed up – seven more than what we'd asked for!

Jeff continually serves as a challenge to me when I find myself coming up with reasons why I can't take this faith step or that one. Honestly, if he can trust God for ways to help others while in a maximum security prison, surely I can do the same in the comfortable Midwestern life I live. Paul did. Jeff does. How about you?

What faith goal are you reluctant to claim because you can't see any way for it to happen? Can you invite God to be responsible for the "how" while you take responsibility only to trust him for the end?

Chapter 20

No Thoughts of Doubt

∿∿

C an you see in your mind's eye your faith goal fulfilled? This is a great test to determine if your goal is clear enough.

Back in the early 1900's William James said that one of the most important discoveries up to that time was not the electric light or even the automobile. "The most important discovery," he asserted, "is that man can change his behavior and his attitude by what he thinks." Another person said it this way: you are what you hold in the focus of your imagination. Napoleon Hill, one of the fathers of the Positive Mental Attitude school of motivational speakers has been famously quoted as saying, "Whatever the mind of man can conceive and believe, it can achieve."

After Walt Disney built the first Disneyland in California, he went on to buy 27 square miles of land for Disney World in Florida, though he died before the amazing theme park was built. While in the hospital before his death, a friend asked him, "Are you disappointed that you will never see Disney World?" Walt answered, "If I hadn't seen it already in my mind you would never see it." That's what visualizing your faith goal looks like.

Of course, our belief in the truth of who God is and the exercise of faith are not built on the statements of these men, but rather from truth that comes from God's word. The idea of visualizing your faith is boldly proclaimed in Proverbs 23:7 KJV, "For as he thinketh in his heart, so is he."

The Bible says faith is substance. "Faith is the substance of things hoped for, the evidence of things not seen." (Hebrews 11:1 KJV) Faith is a reality, not a theoretical or nebulous entity. Faith begins as we picture what God is going to do. Whatever we can visualize by faith, whatever we can see in our mind, is a first step of faith. Then, as we keep on believing, God brings it to pass.

We can determine our tomorrows by the words we speak to ourselves today. No one may ever hear these inner words – these thoughts – but they have great power.

That's why Jesus said in Mark 11:22,23, "Have faith in God...I tell you the truth, if anyone says to this mountain, 'Go, throw yourself into the sea,' and does not doubt in his heart but believes that what he says will happen, it will be done for him." When we speak doubting words in our hearts, it can stop our faith, and stop God from working on our behalf.

After you've decided to trust God, what kinds of thoughts come to you? Here are some thoughts my seminar participants tell me they've had:

- It would never happen to me.
- Even if I did write the book who would publish it?
- How would I pay the taxes?
- I have never been very healthy.
- He has never been an open person.
- This is for someone else – not me.
- Luck has never been on my side.

If you find yourself telling yourself things like this, remember the instruction in II Corinthians 10:5, and "...take captive every thought to make it obedient to Christ."

And resist the temptation to make jokes about your faith goals. If you don't defend and stand by them, who is going to?

What thoughts do you need to resist and replace in order to capture and hold the picture in your mind of your faith goal coming to fulfillment?

Chapter 21

Hitting Roadblocks

∿

S ometimes when we make a decision by faith, the way forward doesn't open up immediately. That doesn't mean the decision isn't the right one; it may only mean that moving ahead may take two or three steps instead of one.

Here's what I mean. During my years in military service, God gave four great buddies who were fellow growers. We didn't start out knowing a lot about God, but we were determined to learn. One of the guys had had some exposure to a group called Inter Varsity Christian Fellowship while he was a student at the University of North Carolina, and thought one of their conferences might be a good place to help us understand more about the Bible and the Christian life. He found an upcoming weekend conference – we prayed about it – and decided to go. Unfortunately, the U.S. Military had other plans for us that weekend.

The 82nd Airborne, our unit, had been named an "All-American Division", so when a foreign head of state came to the country, he or she always reviewed the 82nd Airborne on parade. And, one of these parades for a visiting dignitary was scheduled for the weekend of the conference.

Understanding the military chain of command, we went to our First Sergeant to get weekend passes for the four of us. "Are you kidding?" he shook his head. "Do you want me to lose my job? No one misses these parades except a guard for the barracks, a cook and someone to stay at headquarters. You guys don't qualify as any of those. The answer is no."

We'd made a decision by faith to go; now this roadblock. We asked God what to do, and it seemed clear to all of us that our First Sergeant's decision hadn't changed God's decision at all. He still wanted us to go to the conference. As we sat puzzling what to do next, one of the guys suggested we try the Division Chaplain.

After hearing our story, he stood up from his chair, put his hands on the desk, and said, "I order you to go to your barracks, change into civilian clothes, and get off the post for the weekend." Good soldiers that we were, we gave him a snappy salute and a "yes, sir" in unison, and left at once to follow that order.

This episode wasn't so earth-shattering that we all marked it as a turning point for our faith. But it was forward movement for us in faith – in seeing that when God led us into a decision, he could provide what was needed to see that decision fulfilled. He didn't give us a goal, then leave us on our own to figure out how to make the journey, especially when roadblocks appeared. He started with us; he stayed with us; he gave what we needed to do His will. That was the lesson we learned in that episode, and in hundreds of others like that one.

It's interesting to observe that so many years later, one of the four, Herb Schlossberg, wrote a Gold Medallion Award-winning book, Idols for Destruction. Another, Walter Hooper, became the personal secretary to C. S. Lewis, and managed Lewis's estate after his death. In these small decisions we were making by faith, and in the challenges that sometimes followed as we learned to follow those decisions, an infrastructure for a life of faith was growing in us, step-by-step, decision by decision.

Don't quit if you decide by faith, in response to God's leading, and a roadblock – or maybe several roadblocks – appear. God will stay with you until the goal he's given becomes reality.

Are roadblocks causing your faith to weaken? How can you refocus on God and his desire to bless you?

Chapter 22

Planting Seeds for the Long Haul

∿∿

Recently, I read a wonderful book, *Quiet Moments with Bill Bright*, in which Dr. Bright, founder of Campus Crusade for Christ International, looked back on key moments in his spiritual journey. One of the stories hit me with a jolt.

He said, "Fifty years ago I heard Dr. Oswald Smith, well-known Christian pastor and missionary statesman, challenge a thousand singles to commit their lives to helping introduce others to Christ. He asked each of us to place our names on a country and claim it for the Lord. I put my name on the Soviet Union and began praying for its people. After I married Vonette, she joined me in prayer. Over the years, God gave us a special love and burden for the Soviet people."

He went on, "For seventy-three years the government of the Soviet Union persecuted believers. Thousands lost their lives in forced labor camps and other difficult circumstances. Then at the height of the Cold War in 1978, Russian officials invited me to speak in their country. During a time when Westerners had little contact with the Soviet people, I spoke twenty times in eighteen Russian cities. On Easter Sunday 1990, I stood in the Palace of Congress inside the Kremlin walls and presented the message of God's love and forgiveness to 6,000 Russian people. An estimated 250 million people watched by television and 100 million listened by radio. What a privilege! I spoke to millions of Russians who had been denied the gospel for seventy-three years and shared with them the most glorious message ever given: John 3:16."

From Dr. Bright's gospel proclamation in 1990, fast-forward to 1992 when I traveled to Russia with a United States agriculture team. During that trip we came in contact with one small house church in Novagrod, Russia and along with these believers, gave away Bibles on the main streets of St. Petersburg. As Russians would receive God's Word, their eyes would light up and faces break into smiles. I have since returned sixteen times to help start churches, help open a drug rehabilitation house, and teach personal evangelism.

After some time, there were twenty-one churches alive and well in the Novagrod area. As I mentioned earlier, it came to me that a summer Bible camp would help keep the ministries of these churches alive and growing. I know little about Christian camping, so invited my friend George Cheek to go along as an advisor on my next Russian trip. (George has directed the large and very successful Maranatha Bible Camp outside North Platte, Nebraska for over thirty years.) When I asked him about going, he responded with an immediate and hearty, "Yes!" "There's just one hitch," I cautioned him. "The only time we can schedule this trip is two weeks in the middle of the summer, and I know that's your busiest season at the camp you direct."

"Oh, Russ," he smiled. "When I was in college I made a faith request to God that I might be used by him to start a Bible camp on every continent in the world. Do you think I'd miss receiving his answer?"

In putting together these stories, I could see two believers who had never met – Dr. Bright and George Cheek, each with a heart to share Christ's gospel in Russia, and who made faith requests that they might be able to do so. The fruit I saw in Russia came from seed planted on ground that had already been tilled years before by these two men of God and their faith.

What faith prayers are you praying that will till the ground for seeds planted by your children, grandchildren and others, so fruit for God's kingdom may abound?

Section IV

Let Faith Germinate

Chapter 23

When Peace Rules

ᘯᘯ

In Colossians 3:15 Paul instructs us to "let the peace of Christ rule in your hearts." When we are making decisions consistent with the will of God, he gives us his peace. It lives in our hearts; no force or determination required on our part. All we have to do is *let* the peace that God has already placed in our hearts, rule. In other words, say yes to peace.

I was reminded of this a couple of years ago when I responded to an H&R Block offer to have my taxes reviewed. For $29.95 a tax advisor would check last year's returns for errors. "In 87% of taxes we review we find mistakes," the ad declared. That looked like pretty good odds to me, so I packaged up my tax records and deposited them at my local H&R Block office.

I checked on progress after a couple of months, and the tax advisor asked for more time, so I agreed, and proceeded to forget all about leaving the records there. When it came time to begin pulling together information for the present year's taxes, I went by the H&R Block office to pick up my records – but none could be found, even though they searched everywhere. Had I forgotten that I had picked them up? I checked with my tax accountant and literally everywhere in my house just in case. Not a record in sight

Now what? As I stewed, God's Spirit brought to mind a surprising instruction. "Think of Colossians 3:15, Russ," was the word. "Let the peace of Christ rule in your heart." This was not the direction I was expecting, but since I had no other leading, I decided to simply respond and relax in God's peace. Even though I still wasn't clear about what to do about the tax records, the next day I found myself still relaxed, and even rejoicing about what God was going to do through this annoyance.

The following day H&R Block called – they'd found the records. Life went on. But it went on better for me because of the Holy Spirit's reminder that God's peace is available all the time; all I have to do to experience it is say yes. When I do, life circumstances that could leave me upset, anxious, irritated, annoyed, critical, angry – all experiences that are the opposite of the abundant life God promises – can leave me relaxed and at peace. Difficulties in our lives work for good because we love God and are called to fulfill his purposes. But during the interim between the moment of difficulty and the deliverance, we can experience tension or peace, depending on whether or not we choose to let God's peace rule.

When my brother Charlie and his family were missionaries in the Philippines, he was in need of a vehicle. Vehicles that would fit a family of five were much more expensive there than in the U.S. How would he finance the purchase?

The idea came to him that if he could buy a van in the U.S., ship it to the Philippines, drive it for the year or so left on his term there, and sell it, he could both have the vehicle he needed, and make a profit. He prayed about the idea, asked for counsel, and then took $13,000 out of his children's college fund to buy the van, confident he would be able to repay the "loan" in a year or so.

He purchased a van and had it shipped to the Philippines. Unfortunately, a government official there took a liking to the van and decided he would not allow it out of the warehouse where it had been held, waiting for the owner to pick it up. Months of requests, forms, hearings, and payments followed, until the $13,000 Charlie had originally invested in the van had now risen to $20,000 – and he still did not have possession of the van. When the time came for the family to head back to the United States, the van had still not been released. To Charlie's knowledge, it sits in a warehouse (or perhaps the official's garage) to this day. He lost both the car and the additional money invested.

"But," he told me, "during this frustrating time – even on the day I got on the plane to leave the Philippines – God gave me incredible peace. I could give thanks that God was going to bring good from what appeared to be terrible circumstances, and let it go."

When he returned to the U.S., the Lord opened a ministry to businessmen in Nebraska. Charlie found that this story of apparent failure ministered far more powerfully to the business people he was helping than did his stories of success. "I did what seemed to clearly be the will of God, but it appeared to work out to my detriment. Yet giving thanks and trusting God during those difficult circumstances helped my faith grow. When I told that story of seeing a spiritual victory in the face of apparent material defeat, many were helped and encouraged." Later, a businessman who heard the story wrote Charlie a check for $10,000. "For the college fund," he said.

Is God's peace ruling in your heart? Where do you need to say "no" to anxiety and let the peace of Christ be your steady state?

Chapter 24

Persist in Prayer

∿

What happens when you add a timetable to your faith request, and the deadline approaches, then passes? Do you give up in despair? Does this mean God has said no? Or what about the times when your goal seemed crystal clear, but then becomes fuzzy? Does this mean you were guilty of "asking amiss"? Strategies to meet these faith inhibitors can help keep your faith strong.

1. Have you begun to pray about a goal, and have since lost the burden to see your request fulfilled? When this happens (and it does) I first stop and ask God if I have aligned with him on the request. Did I ask too big or too little? Sometimes we pray for bathtub stoppers when God wants to give houses. Let God adjust the details of your prayers. Sometimes we need to back up and seek counsel because we aren't clear about what we really need.

2. Another approach is to simply put a hold on praying about the request for a while. It may be the right request, but not the right timing. Remember that God has made everything beautiful in its time. (Ecclesiastics 3:11). To me this means the timing of his answer may be a critical part of deciding whether the answer is a blessing or a curse. We need to honor his wisdom in meeting our requests in his timing.

3. Remember our enemy, the devil, is actively opposing us in growing our faith. When Daniel began to pray and fast for

understanding a vision he had been given, he waited three weeks for the answer to come. (Daniel 10:1-14) When the angel Gabriel arrived with the vision's meaning, he explained that from the first day Daniel prayed, God had answered. However, his arrival had been delayed by the prince of Persia, generally understood to be a fallen angel or territorial spirit. It was only after an intervention by the archangel Michael that Gabriel was able to break through the hindrances and deliver the answer to Daniel's prayer. Daniel was not aware of this cosmic battle; we may not be either. But we need to follow Daniel's example in not abandoning our faith. An angel may be intervening just as we're walking out the door!

Jesus tells us in Matthew 7 that we are to ask, seek and knock if we want to receive. In the original language, these verbs have a sense of continued action, not just a one-time asking, seeking or knocking. We give up too soon. Because God is omnipotent and omniscient, He knows no deadlines. We may see our deadlines come and go, yet when He does answer, we see that His timing was perfect all along.

Are there faith requests you've abandoned because you lost heart or you didn't see fulfillment when you expected?

Chapter 25

Stopping Faith Stoppers

ᜡᜡ

Faith can be undermined by our beliefs about our lack of ability, our motivation, the devil, our self-image or lack of time. These things can keep us from praying big prayers, and sticking with those prayers until God acts.

So, how do you stop all the negativity that can keep you from praying big prayers? I believe the Bible gives three very powerful ways to clean the slate of unwanted patterns of behavior, thought and feelings.

1. Drop It
   I Peter 5:7 says, "Cast all your anxiety on him because he cares for you." One of the Webster definitions of the word "cast" is "holding an anchor over the edge of a boat and letting it go." What a picture! When a concern, fear or doubt enters your mind, take hold of it and say in prayer, "Right now I am willing to release this to you, Jesus." You may have had a lifetime of holding on tightly to concerns, so this prayer may take some repeating until it hits maximum effectiveness. Just like breathing in and out is second nature to you, this prayer and the release it brings will become second nature over time.

2. Count It Joy

   In James 1:2 NLT we are instructed, "Whenever trouble comes your way, let it be an opportunity for you." Or in Barclay's translation it reads, "When all kinds of trouble and trials crowd into your life don't resent them as intruders but welcome them as friends." Another translation says, "count it all joy." I think this means when you have a harmful thought or emotion, welcome it into yourself, wrap it in joy and it will usually dissolve. If it doesn't completely, release what remains to Jesus.

   A speaker in Cape Town South Africa changed my thinking about negative feelings, thoughts and emotions. We hold onto our feelings; it is even in our language. When we feel angry or sad, we don't usually say, "I feel angry" or "I feel sad." We say "I am angry" or "I am sad." We are misidentifying that we *are* the feelings, that feelings are holding on to us. This isn't true. We're in control, so we're free to release our negative feelings at will and let God dissolve them.

3. Pray the Ephesians Prayer

   Paul prayed this for his friends in Ephesus: "I pray that from his glorious, unlimited resources he will give you mighty inner strength through his Holy Spirit. And I pray that Christ will be more and more at home in your hearts as you trust in him. May your roots go down deep into the soil of God's marvelous love. And may you have the power to understand, as all God's people should, how wide, how long, how high, and how deep his love really is. May you experience the love of Christ, though it is so great you will never fully understand it. Then you will be filled with the fullness of life and power that comes from God." (Ephesians 3:16-19 NLT)

   (You'll find this prayer of Paul's sinks in deeper if you will stop right now, and read it again, this time very slowly.)

Paul prayed two things – and sought two results – for the believers in Ephesus.

Prayer: I pray that he may strengthen you with power through his Spirit in your inner being.
Result: So that Christ may dwell in your hearts through faith.

Prayer: I pray that Christ will be at home in your hearts as you trust him.
Result: So you may experience God's love and the power that comes from God.

We can and should pray these prayers for ourselves. If you do, God will reveal to you what it means to be filled with the "fullness of God himself." As you do, you'll see some wonderful changes in your life. People have told me about:

- Greater ease, effectiveness and joy in daily activities
- More love toward themselves and others
- Positive changes in behavior and/or attitude
- More open and effective communications
- Increased problem-solving ability
- More laughter
- Greater openness and flexibility
- Being more relaxed and confident, both in action and at rest
- Accomplishments and completions
- New beginnings
- Greater ease in acquiring new abilities, skills or gifts.

When I pray this prayer for myself, I say it this way:
"Thank you, because of your grace and goodness I am in the family of God. I pray that because of your riches, I may be strengthened by your Holy Spirit in my inner being, so that Christ may rule in my heart through faith. I pray because I am rooted and anchored in love, I may have the power to grasp the love of Christ that is beyond my understanding and may be filled up to all the fullness of God."

I believe if you do these three things you can stop the faith stoppers and keep moving toward answered prayers.

Are any of these three faith stoppers plaguing you? What step can you take today to get moving in faith again?

Chapter 26

The Bible Sustains Faith

∿∿

F ort Bragg, North Carolina, home of the Army 82nd Airborne. It's anything but a seminary, but it's where I learned that grounded faith must be grounded in knowing God's Word.

It started my first day there as a paratrooper-in-training. Because I was as new to the Christian faith as I was to jumping out of airplanes, a poster at the Induction Center caught my eye.

Bible Study
Division Religious Center
6:30 Saturday night

Saturday night? Did I read it right? Wasn't Bible stuff supposed to happen on Sunday? Either these people were confused or they knew something I didn't. I decided to go and find out which it was.

I joined five other servicemen in the small room; a second lieutenant stood in front, talking about an illustration of an old-fashioned wagon wheel he'd drawn. Christ was at the hub in the center; above one of the spokes coming from that hub he was writing, "The Word." He looked up, and as matter-of-factly as if he was asking for a recitation of our name/rank/serial number, he said, "Can anybody give me a verse from the Bible about the Bible?"

I snorted to myself. "Yeah, right," I thought. "Do we look like a bunch of preachers?" Fortunately I only muttered to myself because within seconds, a corporal sitting next to me put up his hand. "How about I Peter 2:2 and 3?" he asked. Lt. Tabb shook his head affirmatively, and said, "Quote it."

He did!

I closed my little Army-issued Gideon Bible and slid down into my seat, praying he wouldn't call on me to quote anything from the Bible.

Wow. These guys were serious about God, enough so they actually memorized parts of the Bible. I'd never seen anything like it. So, after the meeting, when Lt. Tabb offered me a little packet with Bible verses to memorize like I'd seen the others do, I took it. "Why don't you memorize three verses this week, Russ, and I'll do the same. When we meet next week we can check each other out to see if we've gotten them word perfect."

I learned three verses; he learned only two, but rank has its privileges. I was on my way to a year-long adventure of memorizing and reviewing three Bible verses a week. As I look back, that decision to get God's word into my head was a major turning point. The Bible began to come alive for me. In the years ahead, as I faced decisions, the Spirit of God would reach down inside me and bring up one of those verses I'd learned to show me God's will. Sometimes I got guidance; other times encouragement, or understanding, or words to pray, or words to share. Those verses, and others, "hidden in my heart" have been the mainstay of my faith.

"Faith comes...by the word of God," Romans 10:17 teaches. For me, faith comes by the word of God, and also perseveres by the word of God. It gives the power we need to keep on believing.

Do you spend time regularly reading, studying, hearing and thinking about God's word to us in the Bible? What can you do to begin today to receive strength for your faith from God's word?

Chapter 27

Faith is a Process

A re you less than the faith warrior you'd like to be? Are you concerned that God won't entrust you with faith victories because you don't think you're strong enough? When I feel this way, I take tremendous courage from the story of Gideon's defeat of the Midianites in Judges 6 and 7. This may become a favorite of yours, too.

First, here's how I'd *like* the story to read. I'd like it to begin with Judges 6:12,14 "When the angel of the Lord appeared to Gideon, he said, 'The Lord is with you, mighty warrior...Go in the strength you have and save Israel out of Midian's hand. Am I not sending you?" Then, we'd fast forward a whole chapter straight to Judges 7:15. "...[Gideon] worshipped. He returned to the camp of Israel and called out, 'Get up! The Lord has given the Midianite camp into your hands.'" Gideon divided his 300 men into three companies, attacked the camp and all the Midianites ran, crying out as they fled. Then the Lord caused the men throughout the camp to turn on each other with their swords. The Midianites were actually killing each other! A mighty victory came that day, for the Lord and for Gideon.

All right! Now that's how a faith story should unfold! Clear message from God, instant response from his servant, rousing victory that could not have happened by the hand of man alone.

Unfortunately, though, this is how the story began and ended, I left out the meandering middle which is anything but stellar. If you go back and read Judges 6:15 – 7:14, you'll get a picture of a warrior who is much more like us than the A+B= Victory picture I painted as we began. This mighty warrior (remember, *God* named him this) made not just one step of faith, but several steps of faith that eventually led him to the victory God intended.

Look at this process and see if any of these "falters" sound familiar? They did to me!

1. God came to Gideon with a direct command to save Israel, and promised his help. Gideon, instead of grabbing his sword, made an excuse. "How can I save Israel? My clan in the weakest in Manasseh and I am the least in my family." (Judges 6:15)

2. The Lord came back with an even clearer assurance of his direction and help. Gideon tried to stall and divert God's focus on this 'defeat the Midianites' thing by asking for time to prepare an offering.

3. When the offering arrived, God once again showed himself in power by devouring it with a blast of fire. Gideon worshipped, but he still didn't go after his sword.

4. That night the Lord came to Gideon again, this time with what I think might have been a task to help build his strength and courage. (Clearly the path to battle for this mighty warrior was not going to be a direct one!) He was commanded to tear down the altar to Baal and replace it with an altar to the Lord. This direction Gideon did follow, though, the Bible says, "Because he was afraid of his family and the men of the town, he did it at night rather than in the daytime." (Judges 6:27) The townspeople investigated, and pointed the finger at Gideon, with threats of death. However, his father intervened and Gideon's life was spared. After this deliverance, Gideon had enough courage to consider God's initial request.

5. When the Midianites, Amalekites and other joined forces to attack Israel, God again called Gideon, and sent his Spirit. This time Gideon summoned others to follow him. But even though God's Spirit was on him Gideon still sought two more miraculous reassurances of God's presence before he'd pro-

ceed. He placed a pile of wool outside on the ground, and asked that if God was truly leading, in the morning, the wool would be wet, but the ground around it dry. God gave the sign Gideon sought. Still not satisfied, the following night, Gideon reversed the request. If God was with him, the wool was to be dry, the ground wet. With no rebuke, God provided both miracles.

6. Now, CHARGE! No, this time it was God who slowed the process. Gideon's army of 32,000 was too large for this venture to bring glory to God. "You have too many men. I cannot deliver Midian into their hands or Israel would boast against me, 'My own strength has saved me.'" (Judges 7:2) Gideon needed to right-size his faith focus to match God's method for delivering victory. After two downsizings, 300 men were left. Ready now to go? Not quite.

7. The night before the battle, a patient and understanding God came again to Gideon, who was likely not asleep! "Get up, go down against the camp, because I am going to give it into your hands. If you are afraid to attack, go down to the camp with your servant Purah and listen to what they are saying. Afterward, you will be encouraged to attack the camp." (Judges 7:9) I find it heartening that God was fully aware that even after this entire process of faith building, Gideon was still afraid, but instead of condemnation, he received gracious support. Together Gideon and his servant overheard two Midianites discussing a dream that Gideon would defeat them completely. So, with this reassurance, Gideon bowed down and worshipped. The rest of the story – a recounting of a historic victory – you know already.

Here's why we explored this story in such detail. We can get the idea that real faith means taking a huge leap into the dark or believing three impossible things before breakfast. In reality, faith often proceeds much more step-by-step. A woman called me for counsel on how to get out of $50,000 debt in four months. As we talked, I found it had taken them between three and four years to drift into debt. I was guessing this might have constituted 40 or 50 non-faith decisions that led to their trouble. Surely it wasn't unreasonable to think it might take 10 to 15 faith decisions to get them out! Of course God could drop $50,000 from the sky through a lottery win, or a rich uncle's death. However, a miracle like this would sidestep the faith retraining that needed to take place – the growth in faith – that would bond her day-by-day, provision-by-provision to the Faithful One.

The other lesson from Gideon's story is how overwhelmingly loving, forgiving, supportive and encouraging God is when he calls us to walk by faith. Gideon's falters didn't bring brimstone down on his head; they brought patient, kind, personally-tailored care and kindness from the Father who was out to help this mighty warrior grow into his name.

Is there a faith goal God is achieving step-by-step in your life, instead of providing a once-for-all, show-stopping intervention? How can you adjust your own expectations to match your steps to his?

Chapter 28

Adding Cord to Faith

∿

Have you ever walked the mile-high bridge that crosses the Royal Gorge in Colorado? The first time I saw the bridge across that wide, deep canyon, I tried to imagine what complicated apparatus they must have created to stretch that cable across a chasm like that.

As it turns out, the process wasn't as complex as I imagined – but it was a process. Builders began so simply it barely makes sense. Standing on one rim of the canyon, builders flew a *kite* across to people waiting on the other side. (You read right – it was a kite.) The string to the kite was then tied to a somewhat heavier cord, and that cord was pulled across by the team on the opposite side. As you can guess, that cord was then tied to a third, even heavier cord, which was then pulled across. The process continued until a cord strong enough to hold a wire cable was pulled across, and the first support cable was in place to create the bridge.

So it is with the development of our faith. Faith giants didn't magically appear overnight. Their faith was built – cord after cord, trial after trial. They tested the promises of God over and over again and proved his faithfulness. Think of David, standing in faith against Goliath. Was this his first faith venture? The Scripture says it wasn't. When he volunteered to fight Goliath, King Saul evaluated his size, age and experience, and refused him. "You are not able to go out against this Philistine and fight him; you are only a boy, and he has been a fighting man from his youth." But David simply drew from his cord-upon-cord faith experience and said to Saul, "Your servant has been keeping his father's sheep. When a lion or a bear came and carried off a sheep from the flock, I went after it, struck it and rescued the sheep from its mouth. When it turned on me, I seized it by its hair, struck it and killed it. You servant has killed both the lion and the bear; this uncircumcised Philistine will be like one of them, because he has defied the armies of the living God. The Lord who delivered me from the paw of the lion and the paw of the bear will deliver me from the hand of this Philistine." (I Samuel 17:34-37) And he did.

I see a faith lesson here. When God asks large steps of faith from us, he has already worked to prepare us through his deliverance in the past. God didn't send an unequipped boy out to fight the giant who had stared down the entire army of Israel, though he certainly could have – and could have given deliverance. He allowed faith-growth experiences to come to David so the young man could build a repository of memories about how God had worked on his behalf. It was this treasury of faith recollections that gave David heart and courage to take on Goliath. This moment wasn't a first step for David in walking by faith – it was simply the next step.

Recently Jerry, a farmer friend of mine said, "This coming year I could lose a million dollars on my hog operation, but I don't have time to worry about that now." I realized that in response some might have said, "How do you get yourself into these messes?" Or, "I knew you were growing your operation too fast." Or, "A million dollars? You are too relaxed! You had better take this seriously!"

However, I didn't have an ounce of fear for his future, because of what I knew about Jerry's history of walking by faith. You see, three years before Jerry had seen God work unusually for him as he committed himself to do what is called "contracting futures." ("Forward contracting" is a marketing tool with which a farmer might see that the futures market for grain is higher than the current market price and contract to deliver a quantity of grain in October at the higher price. The farmer would sign a contract, and would then be committed to deliver. It's a way to bet on a good crop and a resulting better price on that crop.) When Jerry decided to move into Forward Contracting, corn in January was $4 a bushel, but the price was rising. He contracted to sell one-third of his crop at $5, one-third at $6 and one-third at $7. And he got busy planting!

However, during that growing season, his area got an inordinate amount of rain. Corn production was poor, and by the time of harvest, Jerry hadn't produced enough corn to fulfill the contracts. He realized the seriousness of the situation. "I'm about to lose not just the profit on this corn," he told me, "but all my farms, too." I thought for a moment before responding, and the "cord-upon-cord" principle came to me. "Why don't you take it one day at a time?" I suggested. "Every day, you can pray, 'What do you want me to do today – not tomorrow, just today?'"

Each time we've talked over the last three years, he speaks of God's goodness and faithfulness. He told me recently, "My wife and I are growing so close because we pray every day together, 'What shall we do today?'" He added, "It's three years later and I still have all my farms and half as much debt as I had three years ago." Faith for him is – and will continue to be – a daily walk. I think that's God's desire for us all.

What are some lions or bears God has given you victory over in the past? How can you use these victories to add to your own faith treasury so you have courage when larger opportunities arise?

Chapter 29

Four Yeses and a No

~v~

Someone has suggested God answers prayer in the following five ways:

1. "Yes! I thought you'd never ask!"
2. "Yes, but not yet..."
3. "No. I love you too much."
4. "Yes, but the answer will be different from how you pictured it."
5. "Yes, but the answer will be more than you ever hoped or dreamed."

Let's explore these together.

"Yes. I thought you'd never ask!"

God has so many good things to give us that he can hardly wait until we ask for them. When we finally do, he is often quick to answer. We've all had this happen sometime in our lives. Because of his love for us, and his pleasure in us as we come to him, he delights to say yes.

"Yes, but not yet..."

When God asks us to wait, it is always for a good reason. He may be teaching us to depend wholly on him, preparing us to receive the answer when it comes, or simply refining our prayers.

"No. I love you too much."

God's wisdom is higher than ours. When what we ask is not good for us, God graciously answers "no." He loves us too much to fulfill our wishes against his better judgment. God's graciousness in sometimes saying no is what gives me such boldness to bring requests to him. James tells us what happens when we ask amiss. "When you ask, you do not receive because you ask with wrong motives, that you may spend what you get on your pleasures." (James 4:3) What happens when we ask wrongly? We simply don't receive. God doesn't punish us, or berate us, or withdraw from us; he just says no. How comforting this is! I don't want things or experiences God doesn't want me to have anyway, do you? So I can boldly bring him my needs and desires, relaxing in the fact that if I'm too shortsighted or too foolish to see the harm that might come from one of these requests being fulfilled, God will overrule, and see to it that nothing harmful comes to me.

Sometimes in his love he withholds a "yes" until we deal with a sin we are holding onto. Even this is a gracious answer because unconfessed sin does great harm in our lives. For example, in Mark 11:25, we are told, "When you stand praying, if you hold anything against anyone, forgive him, so that your Father in heaven may forgive your sins." I once started a prayer time, and the Spirit of God brought to mind a real estate closing cost of $300. The sale had taken longer than planned, and hadn't gone as smoothly as I had hoped, so in retribution, I asked for closing costs of $300. That decision might have met my need to get even, but my attitude in it didn't work for God. However, when the Spirit brought it to mind, I said, "Oh, come on, God. That was years ago – the other parties in that sale have forgotten all about it." Maybe they had, but God hadn't, and he wanted me to forgive and make it right. I knew from Mark 11:25 that if I chose not to respond, the door to effective prayer would be shut to me. So I figured the interest on the $300 (about $100 or so), found the address, and wrote a letter explaining how God prompted me to confess my bad attitude and make amends. The check for $400 was cashed, and though I never heard back from the other party, God heard.

"Yes, but the answer will be different from how you pictured it."

Dear friends of mine were out to expand their basement and build on another room. They had plans drawn up, permits in place, and finances lined up. Fall was coming and they wanted to get going before bad weather hit, so they prayed that the building would get going. However, again and again, the company contracted to dig the basement didn't keep their commitments to show up.

Over the winter, my friends found a twenty-acre property with a bigger house, better location and good price. They forgot all about their building project and moved!

In reality, God answered their desire for more room and a more comfortable house. It's just that his answer was a different house, not a remodeled version of their old house.

"Yes, but the answer will be more than you ever hoped or dreamed."

Our requests may be good and right, but God may choose to give us something even better. Barbara, a drug addict now clean for five months, was accepted into drug rehabilitation program, but had no way to pay for it. She asked God to provide a job. Instead her grandmother told her about a program that was designed to support needs like this, and which had funding available. Barbara got the money she needed, and could go to the program at once without waiting to accumulate the funding – more than she could have asked for!

When has God said yes to your prayers in some of these four ways? When has he said no? How do you see his goodness and wisdom in both the yeses and the no's?

Section V

Grow Faith by Giving

Chapter 30

Giving Can Activate Faith

∿∿

I believe that giving is the fastest, surest way to jump-start your faith. It opens our hands so we can receive what God has for us.

Sam Edelstein was a very new Christian when he heard me speak at a conference for college students. One of my joys was to ask the students attending to help with the support of a missionary heading to the field. I presented the need, then asked the students to pray about it overnight, asking God if they were to give, and how much. Sam was new to this praying business, but did ask God and felt the Lord's answer was to give. How much was another question. He prayed again, but this time felt no clear sense of an answer. So, he did what seemed reasonable. He took a sheet of paper, tore it into 20 pieces, wrote a number from one to twenty on each piece, and stuck them all in a ball cap. The one he pulled out said 17. After the morning meeting, he told me, "God is leading me to give $17." Good enough. We'd asked the students to make a three-month commitment, so I asked Sam, "Did you mean $17 total or $17 a month?" Hm-m-m. Sam hadn't heard the three-month part, but decided he'd go with it anyway, and committed to a total of $51.

The next week he called me. He'd just received an unexpected gift of $50 from his aunt in Minnesota. This new Christian was pleased and surprised. "Wow," he said, "God did it."

In the years that followed Sam became a missionary to South America. Now his children are following in his footsteps. An act of giving got his faith "clicked-on" early in his Christian walk, and that beginning became a way of life.

About six weeks ago a $21,000 house that had just been repossessed by the bank came on the real estate market. Because I renovate and resell houses as a side business, my realtor and I agreed that $16,000 cash would be a good bid, so I placed it. The bank came back at once with a counter offer of $21,000. I raised my bid to $19,000; the bank held solid at $21,000.

The next day as I was driving, it came very clearly to my mind that I should bid $17,000. (Now remember, the bank had already rejected my bid of $19,000!) Two days later I was walking out of my house, and the Spirit spoke to me. "Russ, a week ago you promised to give $1000 to help with evangelism in Florida. You should send that gift right now." Who's to dispute an instruction that clear? So I turned around, went back in the house, wrote a thousand-dollar check and put it immediately in the mailbox.

That afternoon I got a call from my realtor. He exclaimed with surprise and triumph, "You just bought a house for $17,000!"

Is there a place where you haven't seen God work, but want to? What act of giving could activate your faith?

Chapter 31

Proving God's Faithfulness

J esus told his followers, "Give, and it shall be given to you. A good measure, pressed down, shaken together, and running over..." (Luke 6:38)

This instruction, and the amazing promise that accompanies it, wasn't intended to point us to a *"gimme gimmick"* we can use to arm-twist God into behaving generously with us. God's instruction to give was intended to help us loosen our grasp on the resources we rely on to meet our own needs, and to free us to look to God as our gracious, generous, trustworthy provider. Generous giving isn't an end in itself; it's the means to grow in our knowledge and experience of God.

Janie had decided she'd had enough of the God stories she'd been force-fed at church, so she quit going. Since she didn't believe them anyway, why waste time? But her sister had different ideas for her, and one Sunday conned her into going to Sunday School on the pretense of needing a ride with Janie. It worked, and Janie wound up in a class where the discussion centered on some ideas that were new to her, ideas like God being loving, and God caring about the details of her life. On the way home, she talked these ideas over with her sister.

"That's right, Janie," her sister said. "God really does care about us, and he wants to give generously to us. In fact, somewhere in the Bible I think it even says that if we give to him, he'll give us

500 times back what we gave! That's how generous he is." (There is no such promise in the Bible, but she had the right idea – God is generous.)

Janie spent the next weekend drinking with her friends, and while driving home with the car full of people she had an accident and rolled the car. Miraculously no one was hurt, but the car was totaled. She decided she would be a callous person not to believe that God had kept her alive, so to pay him back she headed for church. As she sat in the pew, she thought, "I wonder about God. I didn't think he was real, but others like my sister seem to feel it so strongly. And that accident was maybe no accident."

So she decided to take a chance on finding out about God. When the offering plate came around, Janie pulled out $25 and put it in. "That is for you, God," she said. "If you are real, I'd like to see you return it 500 times over like my sister says you will."

Then things began to happen. The stock brokerage firm Janie worked for paid her $700 she wasn't expecting as a bonus for an efficiency idea she'd suggested earlier. A friend she'd loaned $200 to months before called. "If you'll tell me where you live, I'll send you the money I borrowed." Janie was amazed. She'd given up on ever getting that money back. When the money arrived, the check was for $400 instead of $200. In talking with her dad shortly after that, he inquired about a $4,000 debt she had owed. When she told him she still owed the money, he dropped the subject, but later put a check in the mail for the whole amount.

By this time Janie's head was spinning, and she realized that God was communicating to her in the very way she'd asked him. She'd given and he gave back just like he said. He was indeed real.

When have you experienced God's faithfulness to keep his promises in response to your giving? Have you thanked him?

Chapter 32

Sow Your First and Best Seed

∿∿

A few Sundays ago a single mom in our church stood up during the "blessings" segment with this report. "Last month I didn't have money to make it through the month so by faith I decided to give first. On one of my paychecks there was a $585 bonus I didn't know was coming."

I think her choice to honor God first by giving and then trust him for the rest delighted him. Over and over in the Old Testament God's people were told to bring him the first and the best of the harvest, what the Bible calls "first fruits." I believe this means more than just money. God deserves the best of our lives – our time, talents, treasures – the best of everything we have.

However, choosing to follow this principle can be a challenge. During the economy's latest downturn I found my assets stayed relatively stable, but cash flow slowed way down. Enough so, that for a couple of months I found myself struggling about whether to give what I committed first, or pay bills first. This "giving first, giving the best" isn't something we settle once and for all; it may involve a daily or weekly or monthly step of faith.

However, it's a principle that has great power in its application. A few years ago when I was in Cape Town, a South African about thirty years old invited me to his home in the township. He had a story he wanted to tell me. When we were settled in his living room, he began. "I had a drinking problem since I was twenty. I couldn't hold a job or take responsibility, and I treated my wife and children very poorly. I was a mess.." He stopped and shook his head. "But then I found Christ, and we learned about giving a first portion of everything I made to the Lord."

"The only job I could find was delivering fresh fish for a market here in the township. It paid so little, not enough to meet our needs, but we had decided already to give first, so we gave, and trusted God to help us. One day the thought came clearly to me to ask for my own fish-delivery route so I could get some of the profit. I asked, and the company gave it to me. In a few months I had a second route, and at the end of the year I was able to buy a pickup. And now," he finished proudly, "I got this washing machine for my wife!"

We left his house rejoicing – and carrying twenty pounds of fish! He couldn't stop giving.

Are you giving God what's left over, or giving to him first? He under-stands the faith required to let go of resources, especially if they are scarce, and will honor you for your trust in him to supply.

Chapter 33

Givers Receive

∿

The process of living in activated faith can accelerate as we learn the power of giving. When we give to God by giving to others, God in turn honors our willingness to trust his resources instead of our own, and responds. But one stumbling block to giving is the fear of "running out." The thought is this: if I give what I have to someone else, what happens to me?

Here's the answer: when you give, you'll be enriched. And, according to the giving model outlined in II Corinthians 9:6-15, you'll be enriched the most. This passage outlines for us what happens when we give – and who profits in what way. You may be surprised by what it says.

The receiver of our gift is helped. He or she has a need met. The Scripture adds that receiver will give thanks and praise to God.

God gets something too when we give. II Corinthians says he gets thanksgiving and praise, and receives glory.

So far, isn't this what you expected to hear? You give – the receiver wins, God wins. But did you know that as the giver you win hands down?

Listen to this list of what a giver gets, according to II Corinthians 9.

1. The giver will reap much (v. 6)
2. The giver will get the gift returned (v. 8)

3. The giver will have all needs met and more (v. 8)
4. The giver can give more to others (v. 8, 10, 11)
5. The giver will get honor forever (v. 9)
6. The giver will get more seed to plant (v. 10)
7. The giver will see more fruit in the time of harvest (v. 10)
8. The giver can meet others' needs (v. 11)
9. The giver's deeds will match their doctrine (v. 13)
10. The giver will be prayed for (v. 14)
11. The giver will be a vehicle of God's grace (v. 14)
12. The giver will receive a new appreciation for Christ (v. 15)

We don't give to get, but when we give we do get!

A friend of mine and his wife took out a $30,000, five-year mortgage on their house in order to loan money to Christians in Russia who wanted to start a sawmill. Six months later the couple learned that their Russian friends had decided against the sawmill and instead had invested the money in a risky high-tech venture. As you can imagine, my friend was disappointed and angry.

"What should I do?" he asked me.

As I prayed, God continued to bring to mind this Scripture. "So likewise ye, when ye shall have done all those things which are commanded you say, 'We are unprofitable servants. We have done that which was our duty to do.'" (Luke 17:10 KJV) I felt the challenge in this verse was not to look for thanks for our good works, or even to expect that the good works we do will work out good for us. I found it especially powerful that this challenge was given by Jesus in response to his disciples' question about how they could increase their faith. It seems that being willing to give, share, and help at God's direction – even when the results of our giving don't work out to our earthly advantage, or even turns to our disadvantage are great ways to make faith grow.

When you're treated unfairly, give it to God. Give thanks to him, and be glad you had a chance to serve him. Your reaction will be more important than your initial action in growing your faith.

How have you received from God as a result of your giving?

Chapter 34

Giving and Faith Grow Together

∿

When I was fifty years old, I made what I called a Future Faith List. One thing on it was my desire to give in $5000 or $10,000 chunks.

That year started a financial downturn that lasted for nine years. During that time, I was able to maintain a regular, moderate giving plan and not much more. However, a full twelve years after I made that faith list, I was reviewing and God spoke to me. "When are you going to start giving in those large amounts?" he asked.

It took time but I managed to put together $5000 in one chunk and give it. Wow. I had no idea what that one step of giving would do for me or my faith. After praying my next giving goal was $10,000 for the coming year. God had used that first $5000 gift to open the floodgates of my faith, and I found that believing for the $10,000 was easier than believing for $5000. The next year my goal was $20,000; the next $30,000. What a year when I hit $50,000! This year it was $100,000.

Now, I pray God will bless me, and when he does, I give what I've committed to give, pay my taxes, and live modestly on the rest. However, "living on the rest" hasn't led to suffering. I've made sixteen trips to Russia to help start a church, and among other things, also had an amazing vacation travelling 600 miles down the Amazon River.

People often say, "If I had money I would really give." Instead, they may find that if they give first, the money they need will be theirs.

Is there a giving goal you've been putting off because you didn't feel you had the extra money? Can you begin to give anyway, trusting that God will grow your resources as you give?

Chapter 35

God's Generosity

∿∿

Luke 6:38 says, "If you give, you will receive! Your gift will return to you in full measure, pressed down, shaken together to make room for more, and running over. Whatever measure you use in giving – large or small – it will be used to measure what is given back to you. (Luke 6:38 NLT)

On a trip to Russia, I was asked to teach about giving, and this promise from Luke played over and over again in my mind. How powerful it could be if these Russian believers could understand the generosity of their God. But how to communicate the verse's meaning clearly while working through an interpreter? God gave me an idea. I acquired seven paper bags – two large, and the same size, and then five more which were each progressively smaller than the last. I put them all inside one of the large bags so I'd appear to have only one bag.

Then, after I presented Luke 6:38, I held the large bag so the audience could see it, and asked them to listen carefully to the verse again – and to watch just as carefully.

I read, "If you give, you will get! Your gift will return to you in full…" and reached into the large bag to pull out another bag just as large, and set it on the table. Now there were two bags of equal size, one representing their gift, and the other God's response. People shook their heads approvingly.

Then I pointed out that the promise didn't stop there. The rest of the phrase promised God's return in "...overflowing measure..." I took another, slightly smaller bag out of the first large bag, and set it down beside the first on the table.

"Now," I went on, "the promise says '...pressed down.'" I took a third bag from the large one I held, and put it beside the other two. One bag (their "gift") had now generated a response of three.

"Look," I continued, "it next says '...shaken together to make room for more...'" and I pulled yet another bag from the large one I held and added it to the collection on the table. By now, laughter and clapping was beginning to break out as the principle of God's generosity began to dawn.

"We're not done," I said. "Look at the finish of the promise. It says, '...running over...'" And I pulled out the last bag to cap off the demonstration. One bag in my hand represented our gift to God, and five on the table, represented his generous response to us.

"This is what God promises when you give to him. He isn't stingy or ruthless; he wants our lives to overflow with blessing. Our acts of giving will jumpstart faith so he can be as kind as he wants to be."

Do you see giving as an obligation? Or as a jumpstart for your faith in a God who is committed to care for you?

Chapter 36

Give the Gospel

∿

I once asked a group of believers, "Think back to your first six months or so after becoming a Christian. How many of you began really seeing changes in your life during those six months?" About 50% of the crowd raised their hands. Then I followed, "Now, for those who saw growth, how many of you saw more growth after you began sharing your faith with others than you did before you began to share? At least 80% raised their hands.

There's a reason why sharing your faith with others will accelerate the growth of your faith. It's explained in Romans 1:16, which tells us the gospel is the power of God. The Bible doesn't say the gospel is a way to get power, or like the power of God, or a generator of God's power. It actually *is* the power of God, and focuses God's power to activate faith.

Here's now Romans 1:17, Amplified Bible explains it: "In the gospel, a righteousness which God ascribes is revealed, both springing *from faith* and leading *to faith* – disclosed through *the way of faith* that arouses to *more faith*..." The gospel and faith are inextricably welded together. So, if you want to increase your faith, get involved in sharing the gospel.

Tom Kotoche became a Christian as a young law student at the University of Nebraska. Shortly after his conversion, I asked if he would share the story of his conversion at a fraternity meeting on campus. Tom debated for a week before he said yes. "I knew identifying with Christ would probably end my political career on campus," he explained to me, "and I wanted to be sure I believed it was worth it." As it turned out, he was right about the campus politics, but as an investment in a highly fruitful life, the decision proved to be more than "worth it." Tom went on to a stint on the mission field, and later was one of the attorneys defending the posting of the Ten Commandments on the wall of the Georgia State Capitol. His life has been rich, full and ever-expanding – a demonstration of what the power of God at work can do as we share our faith.

A friend who has helped scores of men to grow in Christ once observed, "When I first mentor young Christians in *sharing their faith*, 100% of the time I also see them begin to grow in obeying the Bible. But when I begin instead to disciple them first in obeying the Bible, I rarely see them move on to sharing their faith with others." Why? I believe it is because sharing our faith connects us directly to the power of God in a unique way – and in a way that accelerates the growth of faith.

Sometimes we miss this amazing connection to God's power in our lives because we think the task of sharing our faith rests solely on us. It just isn't so. God helps us tell his good news. I remember a number of years ago as I packed for a speaking trip to South Africa, asking the Lord to allow me to personally lead some people to Christ. Soon after, while I was simply sitting on the porch of a South African guest house, my host approached. "Russ, we just got a call from friends at a guest house across town. There's a man there who wants help in finding God, and doesn't know who to ask." Of course I volunteered, delighted to see God answer my prayer. Later, while the missionary I was traveling with was off at a meeting, I wound up drinking tea with the cooks. After just a short conversation I realized one of the cooks had a hunger for God, and I had the opportunity to introduce him to Christ.

Other times we miss chances to share the gospel because we think we need complicated systems or highly sophisticated approaches. Nothing could be further from the truth. One prime example was a letter some of my high school classmates sent to the rest of the class after one of our class reunions. The letter began, "We have a wonderful class, and the way we remained in contact through reunions and letters really put frosting on the cake. Because it has been so good, some of us would like to make sure this extends through all eternity in heaven for all of us. The following is a simple, condensed explanation of how you can know for sure you are going to heaven." As promised, the page that followed detailed God's plan for salvation, and gave instructions on how to receive his gift of love. The letter was warm, simple, gracious, a great example of how easy and genuine it can be to let others know of new life in Christ. (You'll find a copy of the letter in this book's appendix. This may be an approach you'll want to try with your own classmates.)

Sharing the gospel helps those we touch, but from the perspective of growing our faith, it may help us even more because of the connection it gives us to the unlimited power of God in our lives.

How are you sharing the good news of Christ with others?

Section VI

Align to the Will of God

Chapter 37

Seeking God's Will

∿∿

A certain church I know has elective Sunday school classes for their adults. Every three months they choose a new topic to study. The pastor tells me that if they have someone teach on knowing God's will, they can run that class over and over and still people sign up for it in droves. At conferences, if you make one of the workshops "Knowing the Will of God," half the people sign up for it even if there are twenty other choices.

These and other experiences have convinced me of two things: People want to know the will of God, and they're confused about it. The apostle Paul spoke to this dilemma when he wrote, "Do not be foolish, but understand what the Lord's will is." (Ephesians 5:17) Yet it seems that the thing about which God tells us not to be foolish is what we are most foolish about.

When God says, "Understand what the Lord's will is," that's a command. This means that we should be extra diligent on this matter of knowing the will of God. Three things are basic to an understanding of God's will. First, a person must be committed to doing God's will. Second, he must realize that God is working in him. Third, he must launch out. If we have these three things figured out, then everything else about knowing the will of God will line up.

God does not reveal His will to curiosity seekers. If you are thinking, *God, if you let me know your will, I'll decide if I can do it*, God will not allow you to see it. He doesn't work that way. Jesus outlined God's plan this way: "If anyone chooses to do God's will, he will find out whether my teaching comes from God or whether I speak on my own" (John 7:17) What Jesus is saying is that if you are willing to do, then you will know. This is something the whole of Scripture teaches. If you were to stack up all the verses in the Bible on doing the will of God in one place and all the verses on knowing the will of God in another, there would be a giant pile on doing and a skinny little stack on knowing. Once you're committed to doing, knowing comes easily.

One reason so many of us are afraid to commit ourselves to doing the will of God is that we don't understand the goodness of God. We're afraid that he won't make the best choice for us.

There was a fellow once who had a real problem. He was in love with two girls and didn't know what to do. He thought that God could help him, so he said, "God, I'll flip a coin, and you direct it: 'heads' it's Jane, and 'tails' it's Judy." He flipped a quarter, looked at it, saw that it was 'tails' and said, "Okay, God, how about two out of three?"

Like this fellow, sometimes we fear that God will pick the wrong way for us. But once you're committed to do God's will, God *will* let you know what it is. You can trust that He makes His plans for you out of his goodness.

God has a future and hope for everyone who is a Christian for his will is "good, pleasing and perfect." (Romans 12:2) Isn't it amazing that this is what God wants for us? You can figure out some things that are good, like ice cream, and you can figure out things that are pleasing, like doing well at your job. But there is no possibility, apart from the will of God, that you can figure out what's perfect. If I were to ask you if your current job was perfect, you'd have to answer, "I don't know because I don't know what it would be like to do something else." You don't know, but God does. He sorts through all the other options. If we seek to do his will, he says, "My will for you will be good, pleasing and perfect because I know what the other options are."

The Bible has much to say about God's thinking, and it's generally different from ours. I saw this demonstrated at a seminar recently. We asked everyone in the meeting, "If you could find out God's will for some area of your life, what would it be?" The answers fell into two categories – vocation and location. However, those things are hardly mentioned in the Bible. God has a much higher goal for us. "He chose us in [Christ] before the creation of the world to be holy and blameless in his sight...in order that we, who were the first to hope in Christ, might be for the praise of his glory." (Ephesians 1:4,12)

God is not as concerned about where we live or what we do for a living as he is about what we are. You and I get this turned around. We think about programs; God thinks about people. The disciples had this problem when the neighborhood kids came chasing after Jesus. "Get those kids out of there," the distraught disciples cried. But Jesus said, "Wait a minute, let the children come to me and do not hinder them, for the kingdom of heaven belongs to such as these." (see Matthew 19:14)

God has a different perspective than we do. Our big concern, often, is a career. God is thinking about manifesting his Spirit in our lives so that we can have peace, joy, patience, and the other fruits of the Spirit. We think about wealth; he thinks about wisdom. We think about power; he thinks about purity. We think about a career; he thinks about character. His thinking is different because he is far more concerned about what we *are* than what we *do*.

God has a plan for our lives that reaches everything we do: "Whether you eat or drink or whatever you do, do it all for the glory of God." (I Corinthians 10:31) This seems to say that it doesn't matter so much what you do as *what you are in the midst of your doing*. If you specialize on being the kind of person God wants you to be, he will lead you into activities he has planned for you.

Do you think of God as more interested in who you are or what you do?

Chapter 38

God Works in You

~~~

G od works in you to will and do what pleases him, according to Philippians 2:13. If you are committed to doing the will of God, you can conclude that God is working in you. I once heard a man say that angels can do what they please because what they want to do pleases God. In the same way, committed Christians can do as they please because God is working in them. God gives them right desires and ideas. He is inside them, creating the power and desire to do his will. The psalmist knew this: "Delight yourself in the Lord and he will give you the desires of your heart." (Psalm 37:4)

Now, that's liberating. It's completely different from what we normally think. Most of us think we've got to grab hold of God and squeeze his will out of him. But it doesn't work that way; God is revealing his will to us all the time.

For some people, God reaches down into the subconscious and brings things up. Jesus said, "[The Spirit of truth] will bring glory to me by taking from what is mine and making it known to you." (John 16:14) He spoke, among other things, of the Spirit making God's will known.

In another way, the Spirit has direct input into our lives through the Bible. When we read, study, memorize, meditate on, or just hear someone preach God's word, the Spirit has direct input to our brains.

While Daniel was in captivity, he was reading Scriptures one day (in the writings of Jeremiah) and discovered that Jerusalem would be in captivity for seventy years. After some quick calculations, Daniel figured out that the seventy years were up, so he said, "I'd better do something about this," and began praying and fasting. God answered him through an angel: "Since the first day that you set your mind to gain understanding and to humble yourself before your God, your words were heard and I have come in response to them." (Daniel 10:12) Because Daniel read the Scripture, thought about it, prayed about it, and desired to do something, God started to work.

When our thinking is anchored in the truths of the Bible, understanding God's will can get much simpler. I have always admired a simple system to discern God's will that I first learned through Campus Crusade for Christ. Their leader, Bill Bright, encouraged this: if you have an idea, make a pro- and con- list, writing down why the particular decision may or may not be a good one. Then, if nothing on the list contradicts with the teachings of the Bible, move ahead, trusting God will lead you as you go. If we'd use the Bible as the filter for our decisions in this way, think of how many goofy choices would never be made.

Another way the Spirit can lead you is by letting you see for yourself. "Open your eyes and look at the fields! They are ripe for harvest," Jesus said to his disciples. (John 4:35) The international Christian relief and development organization World Vision was founded when a man named Bob Pierce took a trip to the Far East after World War II and saw the tremendous needs that were there. He has spent his life trying to make people see the physical needs of the world.

How do you see God already at work in you showing you his will?

Chapter 39

God Works in You, Part II

~~~

S till another way the Spirit leads is one that doesn't get much credit these days: your own brain. Dawson Trotman, founder of The Navigators, used to say, "The Lord gave you a lot of leading when he gave you a brain." But many people don't use it enough. It may seem unspiritual to say it, but try using your brain. If you're faced with a decision, make up a list and think through each alternative. Suppose you are married and trying to decide what vocation to get into. Your first question should be, "How can I support my family?"

We would see wonderful results if we would just deal with the God-given thoughts that continue in our minds, but most people don't. Let's suppose that a thought came to you that it would be nice to visit Israel and the Bible lands. You should then ask some questions. "When should I go?" "What should I learn when I get there?" "What preparations do I need to make?" "Who should I go with?" But what, invariably, is our standard response to such a thought? "I can't do that; I can't afford it." And the thought is dismissed.

How many people have thought more than once about going to the mission field for three months to see what it's like? How many of them have gone? If this is something you've been thinking about, start asking questions. If God has put those thoughts into your mind, he probably wants you to do something with them.

I asked a friend to substitute teach a Sunday school class for six weeks. He said, "Russ, I'd really like to, but…well, let me tell you something. Two years ago, my wife and I started thinking about things we'd like to do, and I told her and God that what I'd really like to do is be a teacher. So I prayed. And, Russ, maybe I shouldn't have prayed that. You can't imagine how busy God has kept me."

He started going to school, just two classes a week. Then the college found out how good he was, so now he's taking only one class a week – and teaching the other. "Russ," he concluded, "I'd like to substitute but I'm too busy teaching." So many of us have a desire in our hearts, but we never tell God that he has the right to go ahead and fulfill that in our lives.

When I was senior at Iowa State University, a friend and I were walking down the sidewalk and we asked each other, "Why don't we evangelize the whole campus before the year is out?" This was in January. Because it was a long walk to our destination, we discussed it. How could we get to the off-campus students? The fraternities? The dorms? We let ideas run wild. When we got home, we wrote some of them down. Then we talked about them with some other Christians and decided, "Let's do it."

We didn't quite make it, but we did have forty-two dormitory and fraternity meetings, and hundreds of students got to hear the gospel. And we did it through other students. Now, we could have said during our walk, "It's a good idea, but it will never work here. We don't have a full-time Christian worker, and we don't have the money." As it turned out, once we committed ourselves to doing it, God raised up many workers and all the money we needed.

As thoughts come into your mind and linger there, ask God, "Do you really want me (or us) to do this?" Most of us just let those thoughts collapse, and God looks for someone else to respond to him.

You may be asking, "Doesn't Satan bring thoughts into our minds?" He does, but they don't have to mislead us. If we are committed to doing God's will and are grounded in his word, we will be able to discern which thoughts are from God and which are from the Devil.

What ideas have you dismissed that might have been God's will for you?

Chapter 40

Pray, Peace, Press

∿∿

When you are committed to doing the will of God and realize that God is at work in you, what's next? Launch out. Move. Do it. Take some action. Here's a little formula: P-P-P. Pray-Peace-Press.

The apostle Paul said, "Do not be anxious about anything but in everything by prayer and petition, with thanksgiving, present your requests to God." (Philippians 4:6) The first step to taking action is to pray. And when Paul said pray about everything, that's just what he meant.

Second, after you pray, determine if you have peace. Paul also said, "Let the peace of Christ rule in your hearts." (Colossians 3:15) I think of Christ's peace functioning as an umpire, charged with the responsibility of deciding. He views the action and decides what effect this should make in the game. In the same way, once you have prayed about something, decide if you have peace about it. If you don't have peace, then pray some more.

Third, once you've prayed and have peace, then press ahead. Again Paul is our encourager in this. "One thing I do: Forgetting what is behind and straining toward what is ahead, I press on toward the goal to win the prize for which God has called me." (Philippians 3:13-14) Some people say, "Do something, even if it's wrong." Perhaps a better way of saying it would be, "Do something; you might be right."

When you do launch out, one of two things will happen. The opportunity may close. If that happens, you say, "Thanks, God. I guess it wasn't your will." Then back up. The other possibility is that the door will open and resources will be supplied for you to accomplish whatever you have launched out to do.

Many people hesitate at the point of action because they have an ungrounded fear that they will get out of the will of God. But when God closes a door, that's leading, not a lack of leading. If you've told people what your plan is and they ask you what happened to it, just smile and say, "It wasn't the will of God." If anything, only your pride will be hurt, and pride is no great virtue to cultivate anyway.

Making a mistake is not sin. Sin is sinful, but mistakes aren't. When you're committed to doing God's will and have prayed and have peace, then press ahead.

Where might you apply the Pray-Peace-Press formula in your life?

Chapter 41

Ask, Seek, Knock

∿

J esus gave his disciples some guidelines on knowing and doing the will of God that correspond to Pray-Peace-Press. He said, "Ask and it will be given to you; seek and you will find; knock and the door will be opened to you." (Luke 11:9) Ask. Seek. Knock.

First, "ask." This means praying and then remembering what you pray. Usually people advise you to pray and leave it at that, but consider what happens when you forget what you pray.

Remember when Gideon was hiding from his enemies when God said to him, "Gideon, I've chosen you to deliver Israel from the Midianites!" Gideon didn't know quite what to make of this pronouncement, so he decided to ask God to confirm to him that it was he who was calling. "I'll put a fleece outside, and tomorrow if the floor is dry but the fleece is wet, I'll know it's you." (See Judges 6:36-40.) Suppose Gideon forgot what he prayed. Suppose he mixed up the order: "Let's see, was the floor supposed to be wet, or the fleece?"

Sometimes you forget what you pray because the circumstances change so dramatically that you may think, *I didn't pray that*. I used to sell real estate part time. One year business was especially slow. I was working hard but producing little, so I decided I would seek God's will about quitting. I prayed, "If you bless this month, I'll quit at the end of it." That was May, and, as it happened, I sold more in May than I sold in the whole previous year.

At the same time, the real estate company was negotiating the sale of the business. The potential new owner asked me, "If I buy this company, will you stay?" I said, "Oh, no. I've already quit." He said, "What?" I responded, "I told God that if he blessed the last month, I'd quit." The man said, "Well, you got the wrong word. That's leading to stay." But it wasn't. God had clearly shown me his will by answering what I'd asked.

Second, "Seek and you will find." I believe this means seeking information. This is where you use your head again. We are advised, "By wise counsel thou shalt make thy war: and in a multitude of counselors there is safety." (Proverbs 24:6 KJV) That word safety can also be translated "rescue, deliverance, victory." Most people think that counsel is good for guidance, but this verse says it's good for safety, because information is a safety factor.

At first glance, almost every opportunity you come across will look golden. If you're disgruntled, don't like your job, or don't like your Christianity, things look rosy on the other side of the fence. Any opportunity will look like a bowl of peaches to you. But remember this: inside peaches are pits. You need to investigate those pits before you bite into the fruit. You need a balance of information. Get both sides of the story before you accept it.

I know scores of Christians who have told me of the great deal they've found in a multilevel company. They assure me that by working just two years, they can get money coming in that will keep coming while they go to the mission field. Sounds good, but I don't know one of them who has made it to the field. In fact, I know of only one man who signed on to this venture who has even made a living at all, let alone had it support him after he quit. You need to go beyond appearances – ask questions that will give you both sides of the story.

If you're going out to seek information, go to the people who have the experience. For example, if your pastor has never been in business, I wouldn't ask him for advice about going into business. On the other hand, I wouldn't ask the most successful businessman in town to advise you on growing spiritually if he isn't a Christian. Figure out who has the best information and go to that person.

Some people are afraid to ask advice from unbelievers, but I think they can often come up with as good or better information than many Christians because they get information everywhere. And information is amoral. It's neither right nor wrong; it's just there.

Information does not cancel out God's role. Solomon said, "Trust in the Lord with all your heart and lean not on your own understanding." ((Proverbs 3:5) *Lean* is translated from the Hebrew word meaning to "support one's self." The meaning of the verse could well be, "Do not support yourself (make decisions) with your own understanding (yourself alone). Allow God the decision-making power; he'll close the door if he wants to."

Third, Jesus said, "Knock and the door will be opened to you." Once you've sought information, the time comes to knock. Moses and the children of Israel were stuck on the banks of the Red Sea. In front of them was an impassable obstacle. Behind them was Pharaoh's army. Moses declared, "Relax, folks; never again will you see those Egyptians." Now, the Israelites had no weapons. They didn't even know how to fight. They'd been slaves for years. How many of us would have advised them to stop praying in that spot? But God said to Moses, "Quit praying and get the people moving." (see Exodus 14:1-5) The time comes to move out. After you've prayed and sought information, launch out. You'll never know if it was the will of God unless you do it.

Taking initiative in something as crucial as doing God's will would be a frightening thing if God were not watching out for us. So one of the things I've done is to tell God that I always want to be in his will. "God, if you have a file that you look through whenever you think about me, put a red card in there that says, 'Russ wants to be in my will.' No matter what I think at the minute, or what trials or troubles come my way, there's one thing I want, and that's to be in your will." So I go ahead with the confidence that he will protect me.

Where can you apply the Ask-Seek-Knock model to help you move ahead in faith?

Chapter 42

God's Will and the Unexpected

∿

What do you do when something comes along totally out of the blue and upsets your well-balanced Christian life?

I came home from work one day, and my wife told me our neighbor had been fired from his job. His wife had been over, and she was lower than a duck's instep; she didn't know how to cope with her husband's setback. I went to their house after dinner, and the place was filled with gloom.

"Did you like the job?" I asked him. "Yes," he replied glumly. "I'd been there five years, and it was the best job I'd ever had. A couple weeks ago another fellow was talking about quitting, and I thought to myself what a mistake that would be for me. I could see the company growing, and I was growing with it. But the boss suddenly walked in today and said I was fired with hardly an explanation."

So how do you fit that into God's will? You don't; *he does.* I asked this man, "Do you believe that all things work together for good for those who love God?"

He answered, "Yes, I guess so."

I said, "Okay, God has allowed this to happen. The Bible also says, 'In everything give thanks.'" (I Thessalonians 5:18 KJV) I continued, "Even though you don't know how this is all going to turn out, you at least know it is God's will that you give thanks. So every time you think about it tomorrow, and you'll think about it a thousand times, say, 'Thanks, God,' because he can turn it to good as part of his good and perfect plan. Then you also ought to be honest with your friends. If people ask you what you're doing, tell them you got fired. Then tell them you believe it's going to work out for your good because God promised it."

Later, my neighbor sold his house at a nice profit at a time when it was difficult to sell homes. After he moved God gave him a new job in the same field that was far better than the other one. God's will is good and perfect.

This can be the experience of your life as well. Whether you have plenty of time to consider alternatives in making a decision and can go through the process or whether it is a sudden happening, you can know the will of God. But I'd like to warn you: sudden things *are* going to happen to you. Determine *now* that you will believe that God has a better plan for you than any boss, professor, organization, or person.

Commit yourself to do the will of God. Realize that God is already working in your life; then press forward, launching out in what seems best after prayer and seeking his peace. Thank God that his will for your life is good, pleasing and perfect.

What is not working in your life? Do you need to thank God that he is able to bring good, even from what's not working?

Chapter 43

Bankruptcy and God's Will

ᴧᴜᴧ

I t's glorious when we believe and see mountains move. But what about when they don't? What then? For example, what happens when a Christian living by faith faces bankruptcy? I've found this to be an excellent case study of what it means to persevere in faith, even when we aren't seeing the fruit of our faith.

Over the years, I've heard every one of these equally firmly-held, but conflicting thoughts on bankruptcy:

1. Christians shouldn't ever risk bankruptcy by borrowing more money than they can pay back at any one time.
2. Borrowing money at all is just plain wrong.
3. The devil is pushing you into bankruptcy by keeping your products from selling. Rebuke him!
4. God would never lead a Christian to file bankruptcy.
5. If you did file bankruptcy, God wants you to pay the money back—even if it takes the rest of your life.
6. The law provides for bankruptcy, so get a good lawyer and go for it.

So, which is right? Instead of one answer, I'd like to look with you at the experiences – and learning about perseverance – of four different believers who faced this question. Each loved God, was committed to follow him, and sought the counsel of others, but each came to a different conclusion.

Marvin was forced to file bankruptcy when the grocery store he owned went under. Though he couldn't see a way to avoid filing, he came to believe that God wanted him to pay the money back to all he owed, no matter how long it took. Later, while getting to know a new neighbor, he learned that the man was responsible for supplying all military commissaries in America. "It sounds like you have a grocery background from the store you used to own," the man said to Marvin. "How would you like to bid on providing products to us?" Marvin got the bid, and was able to completely repay his creditors, plus move ahead financially.

George made an excellent living as a John Deere implement dealer in Florida. After selling the business, he decided to follow a life dream and bought an aircraft parts company, which quickly became as unsuccessful as his former business was successful. "We had reached a point," George told me, "that it looked like there was no way out but bankruptcy." About that time a friend called George to pass on the name of an attorney who might be able to find ways to protect his assets through what likely lay ahead. In the weeks to come, George struggled with the idea of calling the attorney. "Sometimes I'd even put my hand on the telephone to call him, but I just didn't have peace about it," he said. Finances didn't improve, and the day came when a meeting scheduled for 2:00 that afternoon would provide the forum for the company owners to decide their direction. "That morning, again, I had my hand on the phone to call what I now considered my 'bail-out attorney', but I simply had no peace. Now I'm glad I didn't tie up the phone, because at 11:00 a.m. I got a call from a man I'd never met who told me he'd heard my business might be for sale – and he'd like to talk with me about buying it." George sold the business and celebrated God's deliverance. "I'm so glad I listened to the lack of peace God was giving me," George said. "Taking a questionable road just to protect myself wasn't God's way – that's why he never allowed the phone call I was so tempted to make."

Walter joined two others in starting an alternative home heating business, and got off to a running start. The government was offering tax rebates to those using alternative fuels, so it seemed like everyone wanted to be a customer. However, just after Walter and another partner took on a significant debt load to buy out their partner, the roof caved in. The tax rebate was withdrawn, and about the same time they discovered the partner they had bought out hadn't paid employees' withholding taxes for years so they were saddled with back payments and heavy fines.

Walter pleaded with God to bail him out of this crisis, since bankruptcy was looming. He said, "No bail out came, and one day God seemed to be saying to me, 'Walter, would you trust me if I *didn't* bail you out?'" Walter thought about his answer, and committed himself that he would trust, even if a bailout didn't come. "Almost from that moment on," Walter said, "I couldn't do anything that worked. I had to go clear through bankruptcy, a place I never, ever planned to be." He took a job with a modest weekly paycheck, and worked hard, but it was obvious this income would support his family, but not pay off debt.

Later, seeing Walter's struggle and frustration, his attorney spoke to him with directness and compassion. "Walter, the government has made a provision for bankruptcy. It's a legal option because they know there are situations beyond your control you can do nothing to remedy no matter how good your heart is. They know, and it's okay." In a way that hadn't happened before, Walter heard – and received – the grace. It wasn't the answer he wanted, but he felt peace and rest for the first time in months as in humility he accepted the legal provision for his malady, and got on with his life, no longer burdened with frustration, failure and shame.

Interestingly, he told me that later in their lives, he and his wife received an unexpected six-figure inheritance that restored to them the income they would have made had the business not fallen apart. God helped, but not in the way or timing Walter planned.

This last story is mine. In partnership with two others, we bought a 96-unit apartment house to convert to condominiums. We planned that we could generate income by renting the apartments until they sold, then renovate them after the sale. The numbers made sense, so we got a $100,000 line of credit from a bank, and went into business, figuring we'd have all the apartments sold and the project completed in a year.

That was our plan. What wasn't in our plan was a jump in interest rates to 23%, and a resulting dry-up of interested buyers. The interest on our line of credit skyrocketed, too. Two-and-a-half years later, we sat on the project, now financed by a line of credit that had mushroomed to $478,000. Also, we owed the IRS about $21,000.

What to do? We decided that every time a payment on the line of credit came due, we'd meet with our banker, let him know we had no money for either principal or interest, and let him make any comment he wanted. We could both see what a sketchy plan this was, and the sense of helplessness that went with it was hard on each of us, but it was the best we could generate.

What we wanted was a wonderful, complete, delivered-from-the-deep-waters miracle. Instead, God came, but only in ways that quietly reassured us he was still with us as we passed *through* the waters. At one of the banking meetings, after we'd done our "we have no money..." disclosures, the banker asked, "Doesn't one of you own your house free and clear? Which of you is it?" I put my hand up as low as I could. He looked at me and said, "We want that house." Whew. I sat there for a moment. "My family needs the house," I thought to myself, so I responded quietly, "You can't have it," and waited for all hell to break loose. "Well, I had to ask," he smiled, and the matter never came up again.

During this time we sought counsel from others. Some told us to file bankruptcy and get on with life. Another told us to go back to the bank and borrow another $100,000. "They don't need you badly enough yet," he told us. We chose a third route. We went back to our banker with a simple request. "Jim," I said to him, "you've been at this bank a long time and head of the commercial department, so you've seen lots of business ventures go up and down. What would you recommend we do?"

He leaned forward, put his hand on his chin, paused, then said, "I'd suggest two things. Keep fired up, and keep going to work every day." We took his counsel as our marching orders. Also, I took some time with God to check my own heart during this time. Had I really given the project to God to do with whatever he wanted? I listed what we had: the condominiums, the debt, the unsold projects, the unpaid bills. I imagined all these pieces piled up on a large plate. Then, it seemed a picture came to me of the clouds opening, and that plate simply rising up to heaven. Maybe it was a vision, maybe not. I don't know. But I do know from that time forward the unrest and struggle I had felt changed to peace. The project belonged to God, and we were simply his employees.

In time the economy picked up a little, so we didn't fold. However, it took another full year and another small loan from another bank to finish the project. When all was said and done, we'd made the money we'd intended to, but because it took over three years instead of one, our averaged income equaled what we would have made if we'd each had a "regular" job during that time. The experience didn't end in a blaze of Faith Fireworks, but we did finish the project.

As an interesting addendum, I got a call later from a title company who wanted to share the results of their study of the Colorado Springs market. The company representative said, "We ran the numbers on all the apartment house conversions in the last seven years in this area, and as far as we can tell, yours was the only project of the ten that finished as a completely retail enterprise without having to turn the project back to the bank, or partner with the bank to finish." Plus, I thought to myself, we were the only operation that closed our retail sales office every Sunday. Go figure.

Four stories of financial failure; four somewhat different directions from God about how to finish. Which was right? Which example should you follow, if you are facing financial collapse?

Don't choose any of the four! Instead, persevere in faith and seek God's direction for you, and listen carefully to his leading. Encourage yourself in the Lord's goodness, take responsibility for where you are; undergird all this with thankfulness. You'll get the leading you need, and the grace, mercy and strength to follow that leading.

Is there a place in life where you are facing bankruptcy – either literally or figuratively? What lessons from these faith-followers can encourage you?

Chapter 44

Celebrate the Power of Faith

∿

Let me close with a story that celebrates God's power as he joins his resources with our faith.

During the 1980's many farmers were losing their farms because of the poor economic conditions. As a result, fourteen Christian farmers got together at the National Soybean Expo to pray about how they could help. That little group started the Fellowship of Christian Farmers International (FCFI), with this statement of purpose: "We can't save your farms but we want to help you live by the Bible during these hard times."

Interest and numbers grew quickly as Loren Kruse, editor-in-chief of the largest farm magazine in America, *Successful Farming*, decided to run a couple of full-page articles a year featuring the organization. So, members decided to host a little booth at fairs and Ag Expos to give information on how to join the organization.

In 1992 when Russia opened to Americans, a farmer in Russia asked if a group of Christian farmers could come to Russia to help. I was part of that first trip. In the group were six PhD's, the head of Ascrow Seed Company, other big farmers and me. (The only thing my agriculture degree from Iowa State helped me do was fertilize my lawn.)

Coming home from the trip to Russia, Dennis Schlagel, the Director of FCFI talked about the need for a national convention to draw the forty small groups that made up FCFI together. I had never been on the board but two months later they asked if I would organize and coordinate the conference, and host it in Iowa, since the state was central. I prayed, and God said, "Take the job on one condition: that you can take everyone out to do door-to-door evangelism in Pella, Iowa." They agreed, and God worked; four or five people made decisions for Christ, and as a result the organization's purpose changed. It became: "To take the gospel to farmers and farm organizations around the world." We had no clue about how to best pursue this, however.

In Wisconsin at one of the FCFI trade show booths we hosted, someone gave us 1000 yard sticks to give away as walking sticks to entice people to come to the booth. Someone suggested we add a piece of leather on the stick as sort of a handle. Then someone else said, "Remember the five colored beads that Child Evangelism has used so successfully over the year to share the gospel? Why don't we string those five colored beads on the leather strap before we attach it to the yardstick? Maybe there's a way we could use them as an introduction to talking about the gospel. That is, after all, our purpose."

The walking sticks proved to be an overwhelmingly successful give-away. At the Farm Progress Show in Iowa where 300,000 attend, the people at our little booth couldn't hand them out fast enough. That gave an idea. Why not set up circles of eight chairs, put one person in charge of each circle, let people into the tent eight at a time to get walking sticks and invite them to sit, introduce FCFI and its goal of helping farmers in the U.S. and around the world, and explain the gospel as we showed them the colored beads on the walking sticks. At the end of the presentation we would ask those who wanted to invite Christ into their lives to do so. A simple idea, but as happens when God is behind a simple idea, it worked amazingly well. Three years later when the Farm Progress Show returned to Iowa we counted about 25,000 people coming to our booth, with 2600 decisions for Christ. At the World Plowing Match in Canada, a nine-day exhibition, we lost count of the number of sticks we handed out, but there were over 4200 decisions for Christ. FCFI has presented over 1.5 million walking sticks in the last twelve years with well over 100,000 decisions for Christ.

Walking sticks have taken different shapes and forms over the twelve years. Union Fork and Hoe in Frankfort, New York supplied us with 700,000 rejected wooden hoe handles. Falcon Rule in Auburn, Maine gave us truckloads of yardsticks that became our gospel-proclaiming walking sticks. Hundreds of farmers have bought lumber to make them. Some even painted them John Deere green or International red. Last March I was with Bill Brown, a retired dairy farmer and East Coast/Canada coordinator for FCFI, when we received a call from Walter Powell, area FCFI leader from Georgia. "I've been approached by a company wanting to know if we would be interested in buying some dowels in three different sizes as the company has a warehouse of seconds." Bill and I went to Home Depot and soon saw that dowels in the sizes we were being offered ranged in price from $2.30 - $3.00 each. The next day the company called to say they had over 400,000 dowels we could buy. Did *five cents apiece* seem reasonable if they provided forklifts to load them on our trucks? We took 400,000 dowels, and paid $20,000 for what could have cost us not far from three quarters of a million dollars on the retail market. The company saw dowels they needed to unload; we saw 400,000 more opportunities to share the good news of Jesus.

The impact of these walking sticks continued to grow, even beyond FCFI. When I moved to an acreage near Pleasantville, Iowa, Merrill Goering, a neighbor, stopped by to say hello. We discovered we were both Christians, and in conversation I shared the story of the walking sticks. Merrill was intrigued, and decided to go with me to an upcoming Ag Expo in Cedar Rapids, Iowa to see the miracle of the walking sticks as a way to share Christ. Merrill became a wild fan and talked with the pastor of the church he attended about having a booth at the town's upcoming Fourth of July celebration to hand out the walking sticks. We got a little tent with some flags decorating it, made signs and went to work. Over a hundred people made decisions for Christ that day. Just as exciting, Merrill and his wife Pam caught the fire! They told me recently that their little church has seen over 5,000 people make decisions for Christ in twenty or thirty fairs and city celebrations in southern Iowa. (When the semi-truck arrived in Iowa with 50,000 of the quarter million sticks we'd bought, Merrill stored them for us, and then bought 20,000 for himself and his church. I was there to greet the truck when it arrived from Georgia. As we unloaded, the driver and his wife pulled me aside. "We have to know," they said. "What are you doing with all these sticks?" I quickly grabbed an assembled walking stick and explained the meaning of the colored beads. When I finished, both prayed to receive Christ.)

At a national FFA convention attended by 20,000 high schoolers we have had a booth for years. One year an Ag teacher came to the booth with six of his students in tow. He said, "Last year I received Christ at your booth. I would like to have your people tell these kids the same story about Jesus you told me." Then there was the letter we received from a mother whose son had been killed in an accident some months after the FFA convention. She wrote "I was cleaning out my son's bedroom and in a dresser drawer I found a card from you that he had signed saying 'I know I am going to heaven because I prayed to receive Christ as my Savior.' What a comfort!" And there was the father who came to the tent in one of the New York shows to thank us for leading his son to the Lord. "We have been at odds for years, " he told us. "Now we are back together. It's an answer to years of prayers."

At one of the indoor machinery shows in Northern Iowa three people came looking for sticks. The trio included an older man, one about forty and a boy who looked about eight years old. After they heard the gospel I asked each if they would like to pray; each said yes. The eight-year-old asked if they should cross themselves before they prayed, and I assured him that would be fine. I later learned they were grandfather, father and son. Three generations came to new life in one encounter.

At one of our farm shows it was 103 degrees with terrible humidity, and the crowd was about 80% less than usual. Those that were there were darting from one tent to the next in search of shade. An attractive young couple hurried under our awning. After sharing the Walking Stick Gospel I asked the wife if she knew she was going to heaven. She gave a positive answer and assured me she had received Christ. I turned to the husband; he answered that he wasn't sure, but thought not. The muscles in his wife's neck visibly tightened, and she could have drilled holes through him with the intensity of her glare. Through clenched teeth she said, "You assured me you were a Christian before I agreed to marry you." I was in the Airborne, and played football for the Big Eight, but it was clear to me that retreat was a better strategy than engagement at this point. I stepped back a step and turned directly to him. "Seems to me that it would be a good time right now to make a decision for Christ." He agreed it would. After he prayed they left the tent hand in hand.

At one of the exhibits, the head of the large John Deere display came to talk to us. "What firm did you hire to give you this great idea?" he asked. "We have people in our tent holding your stick pointing and explaining to our people how they can get to your tent. Who told you not to put advertising on your walking stick so people would have to tell others what you are doing and how to get here? It's a great idea, and that firm is one we'd like to hire!" We quickly admitted there was no advertising firm advising us; we didn't print our organization's name on the sticks because we couldn't afford to. Simple as that. I have thought about that encounter many times as an example of the Scripture, "The poor are rich in faith."

In the adventure of the walking sticks, ordinary believers saw – and continue to see – God work extraordinarily. This is the God we serve – mighty, yes, but determined to be mighty on behalf of those who call on him in faith. Activated faith can be a reality for you. All you need to do is to step out and watch God respond.

In the midst, don't allow the struggles you face as you walk by faith keep you from stepping out, from taking risks as you follow Christ's way. God will honor your willingness to express your trust in him. Let the words of this poem be God's words to you – he loves it when you trust him enough to jump into the unknown, knowing the only place you will fall is into his arms.

Risk Taking is Freedom

To laugh is to risk appearing the fool.
To weep is to risk appearing sentimental.
To reach out for another is to risk involvement.
To express feeling is to risk the rejection of your true self.
To place your ideas, your dreams before the crowd
is to risk their loss.
To love is to risk not being loved in return.
To live is to risk dying.
To hope is to risk despair.
To try is to risk failure.
But risks must be taken, because the greatest hazard
in life is to risk nothing.
The person who risks nothing, does nothing, has
nothing, and is nothing.
He may avoid suffering and sorrow,
but he simply cannot learn, feel change, love, grow, live.
Chained by his certitudes, he is a slave; he has
forfeited freedom.
Only a person who risks is free.

Here's to a future filled with God-sized risks, by faith!

Appendix

Resources for Sharing the Gospel

Appendix 1

The Walking Stick Bible

∿∿

The basic message of the Bible, told in colors:

GOLD: Everyone would like to go to heaven when they die.

DARK: Men love darkness rather than light because their deeds are evil and that separates them from God.

RED: God has provided a wonderful solution when Christ died on the cross and shed his blood that was payment for our sins.

WHITE: When Christ comes in, he makes us clean. "Though your sins be as scarlet they shall be as white as snow. Though they be like crimson they shall we as wool."

So if you take God's pardon by receiving Christ he will forgive all your sins and give you the gift of heaven and eternal life with him.

GREEN: Once you have received Christ's pardon for your sin he will give you the Holy Spirit to empower you to live the Christian life. He wants you to grow in grace and in knowledge of himself by (1) praying to see answers, (2) reading the Bible to obey and do his will, (3) share this good news with others, and (4) learn to fellowship with other Christians.

This prayer will guide you to invite Jesus Christ into your life.

PRAYER:

Dear God, I know I am a sinner and need forgiveness. I believe that Jesus Christ died for me on the cross, was buried and rose again that I might have eternal life. I now invite Jesus Christ to come into my life and be my personal savior. Thank you for forgiving my sins and giving me eternal life. Amen.

Appendix 2

Letter to My High School Classmates
∿

Dear Classmates,

We have had a wonderful class and the way we have remained in contact through reunions and letters has really put frosting on the cake. Because it has been so good, some of us would like to make sure this extends through all eternity in heaven for all of us. Following is a simple, condensed, in-color explanation of how you can know for sure you are going to heaven.

HEAVEN (Gold)
God's plan is that we might have eternal life in heaven and an abundant life here on earth. The Bible says, "...and the street of the city was pure gold." (Revelation 21:21b) Also, "...I am come that they might have life and that they might have it more abundantly." (John 10:10)

SIN (Dark)
Mankind has a problem – sin and darkness. God created us in his own image to have an abundant life. He also gave us a will and freedom of choice. The Bible is very clear as to the choice man made. "... Men loved darkness rather than light because their deeds were evil. For everyone that doeth evil hateth the light, neither cometh to the light." (John 3:19,20)

CHRIST'S BLOOD (Red)
God has a wonderful solution for our sin and darkness. Jesus Christ dying on the cross and shedding his blood is the only answer to mankind's problems for sin. The Bible tells us, "…in whom we have redemption through his blood, the forgiveness of sins according to the riches of his grace." (Ephesians 1:7) "For Christ also hath once suffered for sins, the just for the unjust, that he might bring us to God…" (I Peter 3:18a)

FORGIVENESS (White)
God wants to change us and make us a new person to live in fellowship with himself. The Bible also tells us, "Though your sins be as scarlet, they shall be white as snow; though they be red like crimson, they shall be as wool." (Isaiah 1:18)

GROWING (Green)
It was God's plan from the beginning that we grow. God wants us to grow in knowledge of him as obedient Christians. Before we can grow, we must be sure that we have this new life from God. God wants you to have this new life by receiving Christ as Savior. You can receive this new life by praying this prayer from the heart.

PRAYER:
Dear God, I know I am a sinner and need forgiveness. I believe that Jesus Christ died for me on the cross, was buried and rose again that I might have eternal life. I now invite Jesus Christ to come into my life and be my personal savior. Thank you for forgiving my sins and giving me eternal life. Amen.

Does this prayer express the desire of your heart?
If it does, pray this prayer right now, and Christ will enter your heart, bringing eternal life.

It's not just praying a simple prayer, but receiving a pardon from God because of what Christ did on the cross. If you have received Christ, here is a spiritual birth certificate from God.

WHAT YOU WILL KNOW AS A CHRISTIAN:
The Bible says, "And this is the record, that God has given to us eternal life and this life is in his Son. He that hath the Son hath life; and he that hath not the Son of God hath not life." (I John 5:11, 12)

"Activate Your Faith"

∿∿

Russ Johnston's practical faith teaching has taken him to over thirty countries around the world including 16 trips to Russia. He believes God is not only interested in your dreams, but intends to help you fulfill them.

His unique combination of broad experience in business and Christian work makes him a popular motivational speaker. He makes his message simple, practical and powerful for anyone to easily follow. He has authored three other books including God Can Make it Happen, a best seller in several languages, in addition books published by Tyndall House, Victor Booksand Nav Press.

When not traveling Johnston makes his home in Knoxville, Iowa.